My Pag

By Naomi Cla.... allace

By Page

By Naomi Claire Wallace

A catalogue record for this book is available from The British Library

Published by Hope & Plum Publishing
www.hopeandplum.com

ISBN 978-1-8380302-9-2

Table of Contents

Prologue   It Ain't the Size of the Dog in the Fight
1. A City With Bricks
2. Hello, Young Americans
3. A Magician With ISD
4. Pagely
5. Have You Ever Really Looked At A River
6. All About Sam Goody
7. A Short Hike Downhill
8. Two Princes
9. Wholesome
10. Betty and Al
11. Unpagely
12. I Swear
13. Bagels, Oranges and Galas
14. House Pages Can Survive
15. Don't Mess With Texas
16. Don't You Forget About Me
17. Lots of Bruhaha
18. Under Police Investigation
19. Different Colored Socks
20. Aw, Norman
21. Conference Calling
22. Allergic To Spring
23. Holes in the Annex
Epilogue   Now and Forever
Epilogue 2   2020

Prologue: It ain't the size of the dog in the fight...

Imagine placing the United States government under a microscope. Peel away the executive layers and look closely underneath the skin of Congress. Below the intern layer, underneath the elevator operators at the sides of the House floor you will see, just barely, a group of 16-year-olds running around in navy blue blazers and striped ties. U.S. House pages; otherwise known as overachieving, somewhat disoriented adolescents who have left their respective homes and states to spend anywhere from a month to a year running around delivering mail, flags, and an assortment of other strange paraphernalia to a group of politicians. That's the collective definition.

I was a U.S. House page from September 1992 through June 1993. I wanted to go to boarding school, but my parents wouldn't let me. The Page Program was a compromise. I hated high school, I hated myself, and I hated Los Angeles, my hometown. I was a typical angsty 16-year-old.

The world has changed dramatically in the last twenty plus years. My experience was pre-9/11, and though we didn't know it at the time, there was a certain innocence that existed in American culture that has since disappeared. At the time, we could walk pretty freely around Capitol Hill. There was no social media, none of us had cell phones, and the computer lab in the dorm barely worked. We were messengers in the last gasp of time before everyone had their own email accounts. In fact, the specific 200-year-old House of Representatives tradition that I was part of was dismantled a few years ago due to "budget cuts". There are still pages in the Senate, but no longer in the House.

I kept a journal throughout my year as a page and started turning it into this book about a year later. It then stayed buried for a long time before I revisited it. When I first 'dusted it off', I could hear my teenage self in its pages and I've kept it that way. This was my time on Capitol Hill doing something that no one will ever get a chance to do again.

My page experience is a collection of episodic vignettes. I can almost see the *Friends*-like episode titles: The One Where Congressman Pickle Lost His Hearing Aid, or The One With The Dallas Cowboys. Maybe even, The One Where Strom Thurmond Went To The Hospital.

My story exists independent of, yet twisted within, the confines of the House office building we lived in and the House Page School located in the attic of the Library of Congress. It is the story of a girl who learned what it means to trust and to have trust broken. It is a story about people from different states, backgrounds, economic classes, and traditions coming together to share one unique moment. And it is a story about loss, love, and fear. It has a setting with which not many can boast their familiarity, but it has an essence which transcends geographical planes.

Chapter 1: A City With Bricks

The everyday realities of life are somewhat altered when the only brick buildings you see are part of the Universal Studios back lot, and those are facades.

I got out of the car and looked up at the ugliest building I had ever seen. Part of me wanted to run back to the airport screaming, "Take me back to Los Angeles!" You wanted to leave home, I reminded myself. This program was the compromise you reached with your parents. Be a page for a year, then back to LA.

The air was disgusting. I was sweating profusely in the humidity. LA got hot, but never like this.

I slowly drew my head inside and the rest of me followed. There were two police officers at the desk on my left, and a candy machine to my right. I could see people going into the elevators straight ahead.

One of the officers, a tall black man whose nametag read "Officer Rude," stopped me as I went inside.

"It's pronounced, Rudd," he said, reading my mind, "The 'e' is silent."

Having never spoken to a police officer in my life, it was all I could do to respond.

"Oh, um, okay. Rudd."

"Officer Rudd," his voice bellowed.

"Officer Rudd. Is... is this where I'm supposed to be?" I heard myself ask.

"Are you one of the new pages?"

"Yes?" Is that what I was?

"Then yes. Third floor. Check in there. First I need you to step through this metal detector and then I must search your belongings," he said gruffly.

"Search my belongings?" My gaze shifted to the two huge suitcases and duffle bag that I had dragged across the country with me. I was never one to pack light.

"Young lady, this is a federal office building. All packages, suitcases, and persons must be checked," he said, opening my bags.

"I'm sorry, I thought I was going to live here," I said, staring at him as he dug through my t-shirts. I held my breath, hoping he wouldn't take my underwear out for the world to see.

"The third and fourth floors are page residence halls. The rest of the building is government offices. You'll get used to going through metal detectors every day," came the reply from the second officer who had been watching from behind the police desk. He seemed to be thoroughly enjoying watching his partner torture each 16-year-old that came through the door.

"I'm Officer Wilkins," he continued, "Welcome to Washington."

Officer Rude finished searching my bags and I dragged them up to the third floor. The smell of sixty sixteen-year-olds living in a confined space hit me as soon as the elevator doors opened.

The proctors took my name and directed me to room 409, where I was finally able to stop for a moment and get my bearings. I took a good long look at my room. My other two roommates had already moved in, leaving me the middle bed, one dresser, and a nightstand. I started unpacking.

"So what are you in for?" said the voice behind me.

I turned around and saw a redheaded girl leaning against the door.

"Sorry?" I asked, confused.

The girl smiled, "Just kidding. I just meant that you look kind of like someone sent you to prison."

"No, I'm just getting used to everything. I'm Natasha."

"Nice to meet you, I'm Kelsey. So I guess we'll be living together. Where are you from?"

"Los Angeles, you?"

"Michigan. Our other roommate is from West Virginia. Los Angeles... Wow. Do you know any stars?" she asked eagerly.

"No, sorry," I mumbled, embarrassed by the question and my answer. I hated when people asked me that. And they always did. I spent every summer on the east coast, as my grandmother lived in Burlington, Vermont, and most of my mother's family lived in New York or Philadelphia. Every time I met someone new, it was the same question - as if movie stars lined the streets like the cement stars on the Hollywood walk of fame.

"That sucks. If I lived in LA I'd make a point of meeting as many as I could. You know, my cousin went to LA once, and he said that he actually saw Mel Gibson walking down the street!"

I suppressed an eye-roll. "Well, I can believe it... I mean, stars live there, people have to—"

"And do you know that Cooter from *Dukes of Hazzard* is an actual Congressman?" she interrupted. "I really hope I can get to meet him! Oh, and Gopher from the *Love Boat!*"

"Gopher's a congressman?"

"That's what I heard. From Iowa or Idaho or something."

"Wow," was all I could muster. Who's Cooter? I was wondering whether I should actually ask when a short girl with long, brownish-blond hair came into my room with her father, who at first glance reminded me of the truck driver in *Adventures in Babysitting*.

"What are y'ins doin'? I'm Stella."

"Hi," I replied. What does 'y'ins' mean? I guess that's how they talk in West Virginia, I thought. Out loud I managed, "I'm Natasha, nice to meet you."

"Hey there. And you're Kelsey. My pop said he met y'in already."

Kelsey flounced down on her bed and looked at a packet of papers. "It says here that we have an orientation at the Capitol building in an hour. Should we go over now and look around? Natasha, are your parents here?"

"No, they're back in LA. I…"

"Yeah, mine were here before, but they left already."

"I'm leavin' now too," Stella's father cut in. "Stella's mom's already in the car." He gave his daughter a long hug. They were crying a bit, saying how much they would miss each other and to call all the time. I focused on putting some clothes in a drawer.

When the tearful goodbye was finally over, Stella, rubbing her eyes, turned to us and said, "Sorry, I ain't never been away from home before."

"Not for summer camp or anything?" I asked.

"I work during my summers," she said pointedly.

My face flushed slightly with embarrassment. I've worked too, I sulked to myself. I ushered at the Hollywood Bowl, and once was a camp counselor. I had also worked at my synagogue as a teacher's assistant. But how had she never been away from home? I went to my Jewish summer camp every year. Didn't everybody go to camp? As I left my unpacking behind and followed my two new roommates to the Capitol building, I forced myself to focus on having an open mind. We walked outside, and the humidity hit me.

"Arg. It is so gross out. Does this ever stop?" I complained.

"Does what ever stop?" Kelsey asked.

"I feel like I just took a shower or something." I wiped my forehead.

"It's just humid. It'll get better when it gets colder," she replied.

"Ah, something to look forward to," I muttered.

We talked as we walked over to the Capitol building. Kelsey chattered about her hound dog, Norman and her twin brother. I decided pretty quickly that I liked her. We joked around, had similar senses of humor, and were both way too boy-crazy. Stella seemed much weirder to me. She was just different. I couldn't put my finger on it yet. She has weird hair, and I hate her clothes, I decided. Maybe that's it. I shrugged off the feeling. Open mind, I reminded myself. But unlike Kelsey and me, Stella and I were not fast friends.

We were all 16 and juniors in high school. What I didn't think about was how many differences that allows for. Even as we spoke about what books we read or what our teachers were like, it was clear that my private school in Los Angeles seemed worlds away from Stella's public school in West Virginia. Kelsey was somewhere in the middle and managed to maintain diplomacy through her blunt honesty.

Looking back, I credit Stella with teaching me how to be a person. Practically, she taught me how to do laundry, dishes and how to vacuum. Figuratively, she taught me that all things are relative, and to appreciate things such as my private school in Los Angeles. All my complaints up until then were the difference between my father, a physician, and friends whose parents owned major sports teams. Stella worked to help support her family. She had been doing so for years before I met her, and continued to do so after paging was over. She is one of the most important people that I have ever known. At the time, however, the difference in our backgrounds did not lend itself to an immediate friendship.

Chapter 2: Hello, Young Americans

It was good that we left early, because Kelsey, Stella, and I circled around the Capitol building for about half an hour before we figured out how to get inside. We were supposed to be issued IDs, but as this was our first day, no such thing had happened. We were told to go to one door and present our letters of acceptance into the page program. The door we had to go through was underneath the stairs on the House side of the Capitol. We didn't know that; and no one had told us. In addition, they were doing construction.

After walking in circles for fifteen minutes, with increasing frustration, we finally found the correct door, and passed through another metal detector. Then we took the wrong stairway. The building was a labyrinth. Each corridor seemed to lead to either a dead end or yet another corridor. Each of those was lined with portraits or statues. There was one miniscule door close to the House floor that reminded me of the door in *Alice in Wonderland*. There were doors and hallways labeled "Members Only." Later in the year we became immune to those labels, as many of our duties required entry to them. However, that the first day we were thoroughly intimidated.

Finally, on the brink of being late despite having left so early, we found a Capitol Hill police officer who was nice enough to walk us to the correct doorway. My first thought when we entered the House was that it smelled like cigar smoke.

"Isn't this exciting?" Kelsey squealed as we sat down. "The actual floor of the House! And I heard that there are bullet holes in the table over there!"

"From what? When?" I asked.

"From an assassination attempt," came the answer. We looked up to see a tall, proper-looking man. His moustache was curled up at the ends, almost touching his glasses. As he walked over to the table, I noticed that his upper body didn't seem to move.

"This table, on this side," he pointed out. "I am Mr. Anderson, Clerk of the House of Representatives."

"I'm Kelsey, this is Stella and Natasha," Kelsey answered for us.

"A pleasure to meet you. I was a page once, you know, then an elevator operator, and worked my way up from there. Have a seat, we will begin shortly."

"An elevator operator?" I whispered to Kelsey.

"Do you think his moustache looked like that when he was a page?" she giggled.

I looked around at the other pages. A few parents had come along as well. Mr. Anderson walked around greeting people as they came in. Across the room my eyes found two good-looking guys, one tall, pale with light brown hair, the other shorter, with dark hair and dark eyes. They were joking around as though they'd known each other for ages. The darker one saw me staring and waved. Embarrassed, I looked away.

The air conditioning was on full blast. I began to shiver. "I think my sweat is freezing. It's really cold in here."

"Yeah, it is. I guess that's good as we have to wear a blazer every day," Kelsey replied.

"I guess so. It's like I just went from the tropics to Antarctica."

"Settle down, everyone," came Mr. Anderson's booming voice. People were nervous enough to listen.

"Hello, young Americans. I am Donald Anderson, Clerk of the House of Representatives, and a former page. I am here to welcome you all, and show you around. I will be going over important items briefly, but don't worry if you don't remember everything. We expect that it will take some time to familiarize yourselves with these details. My task is to welcome you, and give you an idea of what you should expect over the next few months."

"The moustache doesn't move when he talks," Kelsey whispered. I stifled a giggle.

"To help in this task, I will now introduce you to your supervisors." He turned to acknowledge two women who were standing off to the side. One was older, petite, and dressed like Jackie Kennedy. The other was tall, younger, African-American, and dressed in a more modern-looking suit.

"This is Leni Donnally. She is the Head of the Democratic pages." He pointed to the short older woman.

"Hello, pages, and welcome," came the thick Boston accent.

"And this is Ms. Samson, who is in charge of the Republican pages."

"Welcome, everyone," the taller woman nodded.

Mr. Anderson continued. "You will all be based here, the floor of the House Chamber. You see in the back two corners of the room, there are two desks, one on either side of the floor. Those are the overseers' desks. Congressional offices call in runs to the overseer desks. Those runs will then be distributed amongst the pages. You will each get run sheets. You will write down all your runs and get signatures whenever you drop off a package at an office."

"Like a mailman," Kelsey whispered.

"The rooms behind the overseer's desks are the Cloakrooms. These are basically lounges where members may conduct private business. There will be a few of you on either side who will be Cloakroom pages. Cloakroom pages answer phones in those rooms for the members. Therefore, Cloakroom pages will have to memorize all their party's Members."

"There are 200 and somethin' Democratic ones alone," Stella muttered.

"Up here sit the Documentarian pages." Mr. Anderson pointed to a desk in the front of the house near the speaker's chair. "Documentarian pages will be specially selected. They will ring the bells for the house when it is in session. Then there is Annex II. Two pages each week will be assigned to that building."

A girl across the room raised her hand. "Do we have to go to school, too?" she called out.

"Well, young lady," Mr. Anderson smiled. "I was just getting to that. You will go to school in the House Page School, which is located in the attic of the Library of Congress. School starts at 6:45 every morning, and then you go to work. Whenever the House is in session, there will be pages present. Therefore, if you work late, we do have rules that allow you to miss classes. Who those people are is carefully documented. This is not a free-for-all. You each take four classes…"

My brain trailed off as I stared around the room. This is the House of Representatives, I thought to myself. I work here.

"Are there any other questions?" The voice echoed in my mind, bringing me back to reality. Most people were still in too much of a dream world to ask anything.

"If there are no questions, you will be dismissed. You have the afternoon to do as you please. Then there will be an orientation back at the dorm. Work begins promptly tomorrow morning."

We got up slowly, feeling unsure of ourselves. I looked over to where the two guys had been that I had seen earlier. They had left already. We passed by Mr. Anderson as we headed towards the door. Kelsey thanked him, and he responded by asking us all where we were from.

"I'm from Michigan, Stella's from West Virginia, and Natasha's from Los Angeles," Kelsey recited.

"Los Angeles, really?" Mr. Anderson seemed taken aback. "Who is your member?"

"Henry Waxman," I replied. I had never met him, and the people in his office didn't seem to know what to do with me. However, my parents had researched the program via people they knew, so each phone call was us telling them what paperwork I needed and such.

"Henry Waxman?" Mr. Anderson still seemed confused. "I don't believe he's ever had a page. In fact, I don't believe we've had a page from Southern California before… at least not in the last 30 or so years."

"Really? Well I guess that would explain why his office didn't really know how to handle my application," I shrugged.

"How did you hear about it then? Why did you decide to apply?" Kelsey asked.

"Well, my school used to be all girls, and it merged last year with an all-boys school. When my school was all girls it was really feminist. The all-boys school we merged with used to be a military academy. Last year was, um, kinda tough. I wanted to get away, so I asked my parents if I could apply to boarding school. My dad didn't like that idea, so my mom began asking around about alternatives. A friend of my grandmother's in Vermont had been a senate page, so we decided to look into it."

Mr. Anderson seemed truly intrigued. "I can tell you this much. As the first page from Los Angeles, you now have a precedent to set. I wish you the best of luck."

Kelsey, Stella and I walked back to our building. We went to the third floor and sat in the lounge.

"Well, did you guys get any of what he said?" Kelsey asked. "Other than the bit about LA. I mean that's impressive and all, but I still have loads of questions about what we are actually going to do here."

"I woulda asked a question, but I didn't know where ta start." Stella shook her head.

"I'm sure we'll figure it out as we go along," I said hopefully.

"Hey y'all, I'm Brittany Witt from Pensacola, Florida." We looked up and saw a tall girl standing at the door to the lounge. She weighed about 90 pounds, and at least 20 pounds of that was thick, long brown hair and huge breasts. She flounced inside, smiling.

"I'm just so happy to be here, y'all! Ma sister was a page and just luved it," came the thickest southern accent I had ever heard.

"I'm Kelsey, this is Stella and Natasha," Kelsey introduced us again.

"Where y'all from? Y'all seem so naaacee. It's been such an exciting time. I jus' had my comin' out ball last week and now I'm here."

"Your coming out ball?" I heard myself ask.

"I'm a deb. Ya know, a deb-u-tante. It's jus' the best thing ever."

"A debutante?" Stella squinted disapprovingly. I thought about Stella's father and realized that there was nothing further from her world than debutantes. I had taken dance lessons at one stage, but this I could tell was something completely different.

"I'm from Los Angeles, Kelsey's from Michigan and Stella's from West Virginia," I broke in quickly, before Brittany could acknowledge Stella's glare.

"Ellle Aye?" she screeched excitedly. "Do ya know any movie stars!?"

"Um, no," I eked out, ignoring Kelsey who was shaking her head.

At that moment, two proctors came into the room with a tall thin black girl.

"I don't mean to interrupt. I'm Maya, the head proctor, and this is Julie, my assistant. Ms. Witt, I assume?" Neither Maya nor Julie looked very happy.

"Yeas? That's little ole me."

"Yes, well, this is Sheila, your roommate and…"

"Reeeaaalllyy? I'm jus' so excited to meet you!" Brittany screamed.

Julie sighed and rolled her eyes.

"Ms Witt. I don't know if you are aware, but we have a policy against displaying any material that could be construed as offensive," Maya continued.

Brittany stared with wide eyes and cocked her head to the side. Indeed, I couldn't help but wonder how a person could manage to look so blank. She had no idea what Maya was talking about. Neither did we, but we were fascinated by the interaction all the same.

"Well," Maya continued, "It seems that you have hung something in your room that Sheila here has taken legitimate offense with. Indeed, I have found it offensive as well and must ask you to remove it."

Brittany maintained her wide-eyed, vacant gaze. "I'm so sorry, I simply do not know what y'all are talkin' about," she said with utter sincerity.

Sheila glared at her, and then looked over at Maya who shook her head. "Ms. Witt, you have hung a confederate flag in your bedroom."

If I had not been sitting, I would have fallen. A confederate flag? Holy shit! Kelsey let out a huge gulp of a laugh, and Stella's face became vinegar. Looking at Brittany, however, there was still no sign of understanding. She truly didn't see what offense she had committed.

"Yes? I'm sorry, ma'am, I still don't see what's offensive," she pleaded sincerely.

Maya rolled her eyes. "Will you please come with me, Ms Witt?"

The two proctors, a visibly annoyed Sheila, and a still clueless Brittany walked out of the lounge.

"A confederate flag? Is that really what she said?" I asked.

"Some people live in the past," Stella acknowledged.

"There's living in the past and then living about 150 years ago," Kelsey retorted. "Where is everyone else, anyway?"

"Hanging confederate flags?" I joked.

"It's not funny," Stella said.

"I know. I mean, I'm Jewish, and I don't think I have met anyone who has even *seen* a confederate flag anyplace other than in *Gone with the Wind*," I replied.

"You're Jewish? Really?" Stella asked curiously.

My eyes narrowed. "Yeah, so?"

"Well, I've never met anyone who's Jewish before. You don't look Jewish," she squinted and tilted her head to the side, as if she were examining me for some disease.

That surprised me more than the confederate flag. How could someone have never met a Jew before? Didn't they have Jews in West Virginia? And more importantly, "What did you think Jews looked like?" I asked finally.

"I don't know. Your nose is normal. And you don't have any horns."

I blinked a few times, not sure whether I had heard her correctly. "Horns?" I repeated.

"I'm sorry," Stella apologized, "I just have never met a Jew before."

Kelsey interrupted, "Come on, you guys, we have that orientation thing downstairs. That's probably where everyone else went."

Horns? What on earth was she talking about? Admittedly, I was hardly a religious person. My family has always been more culturally Jewish than religious... The only time I went to services was for the high holy days. However, I was active in my temple youth group, loved my Jewish summer camp, and proud of my heritage. My parents always stressed the idea of learning about and accepting different religious. I even attended a Church of England elementary school. Nobody had ever asked me if I had horns.

Still baffled, I followed my roommates downstairs to a meeting room. Sure enough, it was filled with the same people who had been in the Capitol building. I looked around and saw the two guys I had seen before. The dark haired one looked over at me. This time, I managed a smile. He smiled back.

"Don't think about it, Natasha. She didn't mean anything. You guys are just from really different places," Kelsey whispered.

"I know, it's just... I mean, horns? You and I are from different places too, but you didn't ask me if I had horns."

"But I know a ton of Jews—she doesn't. I'm from Detroit, and I've spent time in other big cities like Chicago. She's from a really small town where people probably still go next door to borrow sugar. Don't take it personally," Kelsey offered.

I thought about that for a moment. The smallest town I had ever been to was Burlington, Vermont. My grandparents moved there from California. It was a university town with a more cosmopolitan population, but the small town nature had been a shock for a family who had lived in New York, Los Angeles, and San Francisco. I imagined that Martinsburg, West Virginia was even smaller than Burlington.

Kelsey looked over at me. "You know, we all might be in DC, but none of us are from here. People are bound to be different. We all might just learn something."

I smiled and nodded. She was right.

Maya came in a few minutes later with a disgruntled Brittany at her side. She ran through fire drill procedures and dorm rules. Some rules were common knowledge, others we did not like at all.

"An actual curfew? Midnight on weekends and 10 on weekdays?" Kelsey yelled when we got back to our room. "Do they think we're two or something? And it's not like we can get around it, they alarm the doors to the stairs and turn off the elevators."

"I know, that's crazy," I agreed. "They're stricter than my mother, and that's saying something."

Kelsey flopped down on her bed staring up at the top bunk, which, in the absence of a fourth roommate, we had begun to use as storage.

"They just don't want us getting into trouble," Stella said. "Did y'ins hear about the scandal a few years back?"

That perked Kelsey up.

"Scandal? What scandal?" she said excitedly.

"Well, apparently ten years ago, a male page had an affair with a male congressman and a female page had an affair with a male congressman. Before that, pages just had to be in high school, lived anywhere they wanted, and went to different schools. When the affairs became public, they regulated the page program. D'ya know, the straight congressman was voted out but the gay one's still in office? He's from some Yankee state, Massachusetts I think."

Yankee state? I blinked. Didn't that word disappear with the Civil War along with confederates?

"He's still in office?" Kelsey asked.

"Yep, but that's why they're so strict. They don't want no fooling around," Stella declared.

"Well I don't want to fool around, I just want to have some fun," I sighed. "I'm supposed to be away from home." What was the use of being on my own if the rules were even stricter than my parents' rules?

"I couldn't have said it better myself," Kelsey nodded. "Girls, tomorrow after school and work we are going exploring."

Chapter 3: A Magician With ISD

Waking up at 5:30 the next morning was one of the hardest things I had ever done in my life. I rolled out of bed, stumbled into the shower, and threw on my button-down white shirt and grey skirt. I was too hot to actually put on my navy blue blazer, so I threw it with my backpack, picking up my tie and putting it in my jacket pocket in the process. I looked over at Stella, who was fully and impeccably dressed.

"How can you tie a tie and tuck in your shirt so early in the morning? And you have your jacket on! It's a million degrees outside," I moaned.

She snickered. "Y'ins not morning people, I see." She looked at Kelsey, who was digging through a drawer looking for socks.

"Yeah, yeah, yeah. Whatever," Kelsey mumbled, rolling her eyes.

"Well, I'm going to breakfast, y'ins comin'? I don't know how y'ins managed to sleep so much with all that racket outside anyways."

"Racket?" I asked, brushing my hair.

"Those garbage cans! It was so loud!"

"What garbage cans?" asked Kelsey.

"And helicopters. You didn't hear them?" Stella stared at us wide-eyed.

"I don't know, I didn't hear anything. I was sleeping. Anyway, I think I'll skip breakfast. It's too early to eat and I'm not ready yet. See you in school." I squinted into the mirror as I put on my black eyeliner.

Stella shrugged and walked out the door.

"I guess it's quieter in West Virginia than it is in LA and Detroit," Kelsey said as she moved next to me in front of the mirror.

"Yeah, I hadn't thought of that." I hadn't thought of a lot of things.

When we were ready, we walked over to school. How could it be this hot at six in the morning? I tried to ignore the sweat that had already begun dripping down my forehead.

They were doing construction on the Jefferson building of the Library of Congress, where our school was. To get up to the attic, we had to enter through the back and walk down a flight of stairs from the first floor to the cellar. From there, we could take the elevator up to the attic. The view once we got up to the top was amazing. If it hadn't been the crack of dawn, maybe I could have appreciated it.

It was now freezing, of course, as the air conditioner was at full blast. I still hadn't tucked in my shirt or tied my tie, but I put on my blazer to stop the sweat from freezing on my skin. I found my way to my first class, History, and sat down in the second row. I immediately put my head down on the desk. 6:30 a.m. was far too early to do anything. Especially think.

The cute, dark-haired guy from orientation sat down next to me.

"Hi there," he said. "Not a morning person, I see."

I picked up my head and shook it. "Not so much."

"Me neither, but I'm doing a better job of faking it. I don't know if I've met you yet."

"I don't think so, but there are so many people that you really never know. I'm Natasha, from Los Angeles, and no, I don't know any stars. Just to save you the trouble of asking," I rambled. He smelled like Drakar—my favorite cologne. He had huge hazel eyes, tan skin, and dark hair. He looked Middle Eastern.

He smiled. "So you've made up your own script, I see."

"It's easier than thinking up a new response when everybody asks you the same questions."

"I hear you. I'm Hani, from Chicago, Arabic, and I hope to meet stars one day. How's that?"

I smiled in spite of myself. "Works for me," I said. "Arabic? I've never heard it put that way."

"My family's from Jordan. My friends and I joke about me being Arabic because they're mostly your typical WASPs, so I just always say that. I guess it is strange if you don't know me."

"I understand. I'm Jewish, and my friends and I tease each other about being JAPs."

"JAPs?" he asked.

"Jewish American Princesses."

He laughed. "Well, JAP, let's make peace between the Jew and the Arab, shall we?"

"Sort of a mini UN. Seems appropriate." If only I could have similar luck making peace with my southern roommate. Which would be more difficult—peace between the Jew and the Arab, or peace between the north and the south?

"Yeah," he said smiling, "My best friend's Polish and I always tease him too. It's not a racial thing. Just funny."

"Do you know my roommate had never met a Jewish person before? She actually asked me if I had horns."

"I believe it. Some guy from Mississippi asked me if I was afraid of hell. I informed him that I was Christian; my family is just from the Middle East. He had to think about that for a while. Where's your roommate from?" he asked.

"West Virginia."

"Where's that?" He hesitated. "Man, I sound like an idiot."

"No you don't. I don't really know where it is either," I admitted. "I've been to Chicago before though."

"And I've met Jews, so we're even."

At that point, a short man with brownish-gray hair and a moustache walked in front of the room. He had a loud, booming voice, and when he was excited by the subject matter that we were learning, made huge arm gestures to illustrate his point.

"Hello, pages. Welcome to the House Page School. It is my duty to remind you that you are the youngest federal employees, and as such, must behave accordingly. I am Mr. Whitzal and this is American history. I just want to clarify something before we begin. I know this is American History, but I am warning you, I don't like wars, so we will not be talking about them."

"Right, um, American history without wars?" Hani whispered.

I giggled, "Is there anything left?"

"Okay," Mr. Whitzal continued, "Slavery in America… anyone? Anyone?"

School ticked on.

My next class was Spanish with Mrs. Miranda. We watched a music video of "El Largo Camino." There were only five people in the class. In English class, our teacher Dr. Mawer informed us that all literature could be translated biblically or sexually or both. He talked with his feet in the same way that Mr. Whitzal spoke with his hands—I almost got motion sickness watching Dr. Mawer dance around the front of the room. Finally, I got to my last class of the day: Math.

I walked into Math and again, took a seat in the second row. Hani came in and sat down next to me.

"You again," he smiled.

"Yeah, you're following me."

"That's what I'm good at."

"Do you want to be advertising that? We are federal employees, if you hadn't heard," I teased.

Hani rolled his eyes. "Hmm. Really. I think that is the first time this hour that I've heard that."

"Yes, I know, I like to be original."

"So, history was, umm... different. I wonder what Math will bring."

"At this point, I'm scared. You know there are only five people in my Spanish class?"

"You're taking Spanish? Spanish, History, Math, English, so you're not taking..."

"Science. Anything to avoid it," I replied.

"Yeah, but this is easy, and Science seems like it will be kind of fun. I heard our teacher almost blew up the Library of Congress doing an experiment once."

"I saw the Science teacher, what's his name? Dr..."

"Mr. Nelson."

"You know the Muppets? When I saw him I decided he looked exactly like Dr. Bunsen Honeydew. I wouldn't be able to sit through a class without laughing."

Hani smiled. "Thanks. Now I'm going to go to class and all I'll be able to think of is how much my teacher looks like a Muppet."

"Well, I'm not looking forward to Math. I'm not much good at anything that involves numbers."

"They don't teach you that in Los Angeles? Oh, I know. Too busy looking at the stars you don't know."

"Exactly," I laughed, "It is nice getting to know other people though."

"Absolutely," Hani said, smiling

Our Math teacher, Mrs. Bowen, walked into class, and announced, "Hi everyone, there's one thing you all need to remember, and that is that Math is your favorite subject. Don't worry about getting everything right, just always show your work and you will get partial credit."

Hani and I looked at each other and giggled. He scribbled something down on a piece of paper and showed to me. *So do you love math yet*? I wrote back, *Oh, yeah. It's my favorite subject.*

I liked Hani immediately. He seemed nice, funny, and more importantly, someone I could relate to. From that first day in class, I knew I wanted to get to know him better. He scribbled funny notes to me all through class. We played tic tac toe, hangman, and, occasionally, did some math problems. I was almost sad when the bell rang and we had to begin our first day of work.

Chapter 4: Pagely

Math class is easy to explain. We all take math, the only difference was that mine was in the attic of the Library of Congress, and my school day ended when Congress convened. It is hard to dramatize the fundamentals of our world, so I fear I have to pause in order to explain the basics of our momentary adolescent universe. First, I must clarify that this is how the page program was in 1992-1993. It was a Democratic house and a Democratic Senate. Bush Sr. was president in the fall, but Clinton was inaugurated in January.

Every year, each side of the house, Republican and Democrat, were allotted a specific number of pages for that specific year. The majority party, the Democrats at the time, had 54 pages and the Republicans had 12. All the Republican pages were there for the school year. The lengths of terms for the Democratic pages varied. Hani, I learned, was a Rostenkowski page. Congressman Rostenkowski always had two pages that went to a school called Gordon Tech in Chicago. Rostenkowski pages were there for the full school year. A few years after I was a page, Rostenkowski was convicted of fraud and lost his seat in Congress. Nine other Democratic pages, including Stella and myself, had yearlong appointments. Initially we were supposed to only be there for one semester, but as there were spring openings, we had gotten extensions.

The pages from Spokane in Washington State were pages for Speaker Foley. Some of them worked in his office. Two pages each week were shipped off to work in annex 2, an office building far away which had its own mini page office. The overseers sat at their desks on the floor and assigned the runs. Floor pages took deliveries only within the capital building. Cloakroom pages answered phones for the congressmen on the floor. Documentarians rang the bells and sat up near the speaker. The rest of us ran all sorts of errands, most of which involved delivering mail. Pages also delivered flags. Constituents could ask their congressmen for a flag that had been flown over the Capitol building. There was a whole room in the basement of the capital, the flag room, which filled that purpose. Pages delivered the flags to and from the offices.

Some of the people we lived with were Senate pages. They worked on the Senate floor and delivered messages on the Senate side of the hill. We didn't see too much of them during the day, but sometimes, if we had a delivery that went to a senator, we bumped into them. There were only about twenty each semester that lived with us, but there were additional Senate pages who worked for Senator Strom Thurmond who lived and went to school elsewhere. They didn't go to the Senate Page School either. We met a few of them the first day. They were office pages and rotated monthly. One was named Thurmond and another was named Strom. They all seemed to be related to each other. In addition, Strom Thurmond had two pages that stayed all year, and a few that rotated after a couple of months. Most Senate pages did live with us. The Senate pages went to a different school in the attic of the Library of Congress: the Senate Page School. In total, House and Senate pages combined, over 150 sixteen and seventeen-year-olds from nearly every state came and went from our building that year.

There were five House office buildings: Cannon, Longworth, Rayburn, Annex one, and Annex two. Rayburn was the nicest and had a subway train to and from the capital. Cannon was the oldest. We also delivered mail to all three Library of Congress buildings, and the three Senate buildings: Dirkson, Hart, and Russell. With the exception of the annex buildings, they were all connected by an intricate series of tunnels that radiated out of the Capitol. If a page didn't take any deliveries to annex 1 (or annex 2 but those runs went on a shuttle to the annex 2 pages), you could spend the entire day inside and underground. Every entrance and exit to every building meant going through a metal detector.

There was a point system to ensure that the pages who did the most runs were rewarded. In addition, the point system functioned to make sure that everyone was working as hard as they could. Runs that were the furthest away (Senate Hart) were worth the most. Each flag counted as a point, even if they were going to the same place. Flags were in big boxes; bulky and annoying to carry for the miles we walked every day. Otherwise, it was the number of deliveries that counted. The pages with the largest number of points got to go home early. The point system only applied to pages that went on runs. Cloakroom, Overseer, Documetarian, and Floor pages were bound to work for the full day regardless. Late in the spring especially, I would race to the floor from school to get the big runs so that I could try to leave early.

It might seem confusing, but call to mind that microscopic layer of the United States government. In context, everything you know about the U.S. political system dictated our daily activities. It was a political bubble of a world, separated by metal detectors and Capitol Hill policemen to contain only us. It was a world where labels such as Democrat, Republican, Conservative, and Liberal helped to define us as people. Those labels came to define our friendships and encouraged adversaries.

Chapter 5: Have You Ever Really Looked At A River

We went from school to work, showing each book to the security guards on the way out, just in case we might have taken one from the reading room. That first day, we walked outside. Later, we learned how to use the underground tunnels to get from school to the Capitol.

Kelsey, Stella and I caught up to each other on the walk over.

"So, I have not seen one cute guy here," Kelsey said matter of factly.

I blushed while Stella nodded in agreement.

"So where are we going later?" I asked.

"Well, I was here a few years ago and we went to this mall - Pentagon City or Crystal City or something. We can go there."

"Sounds good to me," I agreed.

We found our way to the House floor where we were all assigned jobs. Kelsey was assigned to the Ways and Means committee, which meant that she got to work in an office. I didn't really know what else it meant. She reported to them every day, didn't have to do runs, and filled in for their receptionist at lunchtime. I also don't know how she managed to get that job. It seemed random, but it also afforded her privileges, such as working the inauguration in January, that most of us didn't have. Kelsey was really personable, however, and her frankness did her credit. She always appeared on the ball no matter what, and was able to mulit-task without ever seeming frantic. I, on the other hand, tied my tie and tucked in my shirt ~~in~~ on the way to work. I was also from Los Angeles, somewhere foreign to many of the capital hill employees. I was constantly reminded that there had never been a page from LA before. As this was the height of the "Beverly Hills, 90210" craze, my valley girl presence in Washington was regarded as an enigma[1].

The first run I was given involved delivering flags from an office in Rayburn to the capital. I found the office easily enough, picked up the order, and headed back to the Rayburn subway. I waited in line to walk through the metal detector.

"Let me see those boxes," came the policeman's voice.

Surprised, I handed him the 12 big flag boxes that I had spent the better part of the journey finding a way to balance. I watched in astonishment as he opened each box.

"They're just flags," I muttered.

"Young lady, my name is Officer Simpson. It is my job to make sure that no illegal substances pass this way."

"So, you check each of the flags?" I asked before I could stop myself. I wondered silently if he was friends with Officer Rude.

He glared at me as if I was public enemy number one. "You can never be too careful."

---

[1] Just as a side note – Monica Lewinsky was an intern. Not a page. Other than the typical tourist areas, I was not allowed in the white house. When the scandal broke out I found myself constantly saying, "No, that is not what I did. She was not a page."

When he was thoroughly convinced that my flags held no great threat to the union, he thrust them back at me; and I promptly dropped them. Embarrassed, and now holding up the line to the subway, I hurriedly picked up the boxes and tried to find my balance again.

"So, first day's going well, I take it," came a voice from behind me.

Surprised, I looked around to see Hani standing there smiling. He was holding a few envelopes. The light haired guy stood next to him laughing.

I went from pink to bright red. "Yeah, can't you tell?" I muttered.

"Let me help you with those." The light-haired guy bent down and helped me pick up the unwieldy flags. Hani continued to laugh as he watched his friend and me pick up all my flags.

"I'm Dean," the light-haired guy said.

"Nice to meet you, I'm Natasha."

Hani stood watching as Dean and I finally got my flags and me safely in the subway.

Once we were sitting down, I asked, "Do you two know each other from before?"

"We both go to the same high school. Our congressman has two pages from there every year," Hani answered.

"Yeah. Naaaa-taaaaaa-sssssssshhhaaaa, right?" Dean said smiling.

"Don't pay attention to him, he's Polish," Hani laughed.

"Listen to the Arab. You have too much hair to order me around."

"Hmm, interesting…. Hahem. Polish."

Feeling slightly uncomfortable, I interrupted, "Hani told me you guys always tease each other about your nationalities."

"Yeah, he knows I'm joking," Dean said with a wink.

"And I know he smells," Hani chimed in. "Yeah, sorry, you'll get used to us. We go to the same school, now we're roommates, we know each other way too well."

"You're roommates?" I asked.

"I don't think they did that on purpose. Unless they thought that no one else would be able to stand living with him," Dean shrugged, his eyes twinkling.

"We got really lost in Rayburn. How have you been doing?" Hani asked.

"Fine in terms of finding my way. Not so fine in the whole flag department."

"Yeah, that's kinda obvious," Dean teased.

The subway stopped. Dean and Hani headed towards the elevator to go back to the floor.

"See you later then," Hani called after me.

"Yeah, later." I turned to walk up from the sub-basement to the basement to take my flags to the flag room.

"Watch those flags," Dean yelled as I wobbled away.

I rolled my eyes. It took a few extra minutes for me to find the flag office which was near what we called the Page Cloakroom. Both were located in the deepest darkest corner of the labyrinth—otherwise known as the Capital building's basement. I delivered my flags and waited for an elevator. One opened, and the elevator operator took a good look at me before saying, "New page, right?"

"Yeah. I'm Natasha."

"Hi. I'm Jane. Welcome to the Hill."

"Have you been here long?"

She looked at me intently for a moment before responding, "I was a page. Take my advice, keep your eyes and ears open and your mouth shut. Second floor, doors open. Honey, this is your stop."

Chapter 6: All About Sam Goody

That afternoon we were too tired to go anywhere. That night I thought about how out of place I felt. I didn't think I looked much different than everyone else, but it seemed like everyone stared at me as though I was from a different planet. Especially Stella. At the time, I was going through an alternative music phase. My style at the time was grunge, and I dressed accordingly. When not in uniform, I sported flannel shirts, bell-bottom used jeans, and variations on rock type shirts. My shoes were either Doc Martins or Birkenstocks. I thought I was the epitome of fashion, and according to Los Angeles standards at the time, I was. However, I most definitely did not look comfortable in my blazer and tie, and although I had worn uniforms to school my entire life, this particular combination did not allow for the thick necklaces, Doc Martin boots, and black eyeliner that I attempted to pair with it. In addition, I had dirty blond hair which I wore down all the time, and which always seemed to look messy.

For the most part, the fall pages were such an eclectic group that my appearance fit in to a certain extent with my peers. However, they all seemed to fit into the DC machine much better than I did. Stella especially seemed born to wear a blazer and tie. When I complained about dropping my flags, she only looked at me disapprovingly and muttered something about being less careless. Her side of the room was spotless, whereas I threw my clothes into piles which meant I always looked slightly wrinkled. –Stella ironed her shirts every night until they could practically stand up by themselves. I watched her, never having ironed anything in my life.

The next day, Kelsey, Stella and I decided to take our journey off the Hill towards the mall. We got horribly lost in Crystal City before realizing that the mall was actually in Pentagon City. We breathed a sigh of relief when the huge shopping center greeted us as we left the metro station. We had finally reached our Mecca.

I began running through my mental shopping list. "I need to get more socks," I announced while we were on the escalator. "I'm running low."

"Why do you want to buy more?" Stella asked. "Just do laundry."

I looked down at the floor for a moment without answering.

"You do know how to do laundry, don't you?" Stella's eyes squinted disapprovingly.

"Umm... not really. I've um... kinda had..."

"Your mom's done your laundry your whole life."

"More like my housekeeper." I muttered, embarrassed.

Stella rolled her eyes. "When we get back, I'm teaching the spoiled brat over here how to do laundry."

I lowered my head as far as it would go.

"What about dishes?" she demanded. Her voice was iron.

"I've washed dishes before," I said defensively.

"Uh huh. Whatever."

"I—"

"Come on, let's get some stuff to decorate our room," Kelsey interrupted. If she hadn't been there,

Stella and I would probably have bickered the whole time. Whenever we went into a store, the glares I felt coming at me from Stella's direction could have cut ice.

"I don't wanna waste money on such stupid crap," she repeated every time I thought about buying something. "The spoiled brat can if she wants."

Kelsey stepped in diplomatically every time our arguments began. Our last stop was to look for posters at Suncoast Video. I bought some, but on the way out the salesperson went after us.

"Hey, wait a minute," he called out.

We turned around. Had we forgotten to pay for something?

"Where are you girls from? I don't think I've seen y'all here before."

"No, you haven't," Kelsey answered, batting her eyelashes. "We're pages. We just got here. I'm Kelsey, from Michigan, this is Natasha from Los Angeles, and Stella from West Virginia. What's your name?" Kelsey was all smiles as she answered. I wondered if we could quit with the geographical labels that seemed to accompany each introduction.

"I'm Chet. Wow, y'all are from really far away. I bet you haven't met anyone from around here."

"No, not really, just the people in our building," Kelsey flirted with her hand on her hip.

"Well, my friend is having this party on Saturday. If y'all want to come, I'm a senior over at Wakefield High School in Virginia. I have a van so I can pick y'all up."

I looked at him. He was short with a round face and greasy hair but had a friendly eager look about him. Although I wasn't so keen on getting into some strange guy's van, it was nice talking to someone that was not one of the youngest federal employees. I also liked the idea of going to a local party.

"That'd be fun. Hey, there are loads more of us; can a few of us go?" Kelsey asked.

"Sure, it's a big van. Here's my number; give me yours, and I'll call you tomorrow."

Kelsey gave him our number and we chattered the whole way home about how Chet wasn't that cute but maybe he had a friend who was.

When we got to the dorm, a few of the pages were sitting in the lounge: Brittany, Katrina from Washington State, and Jack, another page from Chicago. I had met Katrina and Jack briefly. Katrina was a speaker page and spent most of the time in the Speaker's office. She had long blond hair and was as skinny as Brittany, only without the big boobs. Jack acted more grunge than I did, which was a relief. His hair was longer than most of the other guys in the program, and everything was "dude" this and "dude" that. He loved literature and even though his home was Chicago, had lived all over the place.

"So do you guys want to go to a party Saturday night?" Kelsey asked.

"Hell's yeah!" screamed Brittany, momentarily forgetting the fact that she was a southern debutante. "Whose party?"

"This guy we met at the mall." Kelsey shrugged.

"That sounds good," Katrina said.

"But dude, some guy you met at the mall? Do

you know him or anything?" Jack asked. "I think I need to go along just to keep you girls like, you know, safe and everything."

I stared at Jack, unsure whether to laugh or not. Although he was six feet tall, he weighed about 100 pounds. "Thanks. You're welcome to come, but I'm sure we won't need protection."

A tall girl with curly hair walked in. "Hey guys," she said loudly. "I don't think I've met you yet. I'm Gretl. Like in the *Sound of Music*. I'm from Pigeon, Michigan. It's here." She held up her hand and pointed to the top of her thumb.

"It's on your thumb?" I asked blankly.

Kelsey shook her head at me. "Ignore her. She's from LA. And she doesn't know any stars. Natasha, Michigan is shaped like a hand."

"Yeah, and Pigeon is really small. It's here." Gretl pointed at her thumb again. I nodded, trying to picture Michigan on a US map.

"Y'all, I just can't wait to meet some hotties. Gretl, we're all goin' to a party Saturday night," Brittany interrupted my geography lesson.

"What about the curfew?" Gretl asked.

"We'll be back by midnight," Kelsey replied.

Gretl shrugged. "I don't think I'm going to go. But have fun, you guys!"

It was a group of 12 that piled into Chet's van Saturday night. Most of the group distributed themselves among the guys at the party. Katrina was talking to a guy named Gus, and Kelsey was off with someone named Ben. Stella had opted out of coming. I wasn't surprised. Although she had spent the better part of Saturday teaching me how to do laundry, we didn't talk much when Kelsey wasn't around. Brittany spent the party flirting with every other guy in the room. Jack and I were talking to Chet when we looked at a clock. It was after 11pm.

"Holy shit!" I exclaimed. "We have to get back. Curfew's in less than an hour."

"Curfew?" Chet asked.

"Yeah, dude, they lock the doors to the stairs and alarm the elevators at midnight on weekends," Jack added, worried. "Ten on weekdays. Isn't that crazy?"

"Do you have a phone here somewhere? Jack, if you round everyone up, I'll call and tell them we're running late," I decided.

The proctors were not happy with my tale of traffic woes and missed taxis. I wasn't even buying my own story, but it was good enough for us to get in the building as we arrived back at the dorm at 12:21. We were told in no uncertain terms that this was never to happen again, we were all checked for any possible alcohol consumption, and we were shuttled up to our rooms.

"He was sooo cute!" Kelsey cooed. "He was so sweet and asked me out for next weekend."

"What was his name?" Stella's friend Janie had begun to make a home in our room. She was also from Michigan, and didn't get along with her roommates, so she had decided to adopt us.

"Ben. He's 15, a sophomore, so he's a year younger than me, but he's really nice." The smile on Kelsey's face hadn't faded.

"He was really cute," I agreed, "So was that guy

Katrina was talking to… Gus? Or something?"

"Oh, who was Katrina talking to?" Janie asked, "What did he look like?"

"Brown hair, tan skin. He was cute too."

"Ben was cuter. Blue eyes, sandy brown hair…" Kelsey interjected dreamily.

"Yeah, the blue eyes are a definite plus," I agreed.

Kelsey flung herself onto the bed in a lovelorn pose. I rolled my eyes and began getting ready for bed. Stella and Janie went back to whatever they were talking about before. Janie had short light brown hair, brown eyes and wore glasses. She and Stella had most of their classes together and spent loads of time doing their homework. I couldn't imagine what homework actually, as I found school so incredibly easy. That added to the chasm that was developing between Stella and myself. Her school had been much easier, even though she was in all honors classes. My school had been much harder, without a real honors option. My school simply offered Advanced Placement (AP) or standard. Though even the non-AP, were AP level classes. I had taken the AP European History exam and scored a 5 my sophomore year, without actually taking an AP class.

I still wonder how anyone found the House Page School difficult. I didn't do much work all year and maintained an A-/B+ average. I guess if I had actually tried, I would have gotten straight A's, but I couldn't be bothered. There was too much that was new and exciting to pay that much attention to school. In retrospect, however, I determined it was the fact that the school had to cater to those such as myself who came from private college prep backgrounds, as well as people like Stella who, although she excelled in her school's advanced classes, attended a small rural public school. The result was somewhere in the middle - easy for me, hard for Stella. I believe that Stella was innately brighter than me. The difference found itself lodged in opportunities. She deserved the opportunities that I had, and that I didn't appreciate until I met her.

As I moved some of my books aside to find my pajamas, a note fell out of my math book.

"Huh. I don't think that was there before," I said out loud. Thankfully, no one was paying any attention, so I sat down and opened it.

So, do you think I'm cute?

It wasn't signed, but it didn't have to be. I saw that handwriting every day. Twice each day. I had a silly grin on my face as I thought about what I'd say to Hani the next day. I desperately wanted to know if he liked me. He always made me laugh. I loved seeing him in class every day, and wished that I got to see him more outside of school. He spent most of his time with Dean, and I spent my time with Kelsey.

He's so cute. I bet he does like me. Why else would he write that? And he understands me. So much more than everyone else around here, I thought. I lay down in bed and let myself dream about Hani.

Chapter 7: A Short Hike Downhill

"Part of the page program is getting to know Washington, DC, the capital of your country. In the spirit of this, we have devised the Washington Interscholastic Program, or WISP, which includes a field trip every other Saturday. This Saturday, you will focus on getting to know each other. We will be going on a short downhill hike that will last about an hour in the Shenandoah Mountains. We will arrive at a cabin where a troupe called Interquest will be helping you build yourselves as a team."

Mr. Whitzal's booming voice paused for a moment to survey the tired reactions from the class.

"We will be meeting in the lobby of the dorm at 7:30 a.m. Any questions?"

We all groaned collectively. Waking up at 5:30 every morning was hard enough. Now we had to wake up early on Saturday too? To go on a hike?

"I hate hiking," I whispered to Hani. "I'm the ultimate city person, and a total klutz."

"Aww, it'll be fun. And short. Only an hour," he replied.

"Yeah, but I sprained my ankle about three weeks before I came here. I don't know if a hike is the best idea."

Hani thought about that for a moment. "Tell him," he finally said. "Maybe he'll let you meet us at the cabin or something."

At the end of class I went to Mr. Whitzal to say as much.

"No, no, no. It will be fine. It is a short hike. You will have no problems," he waved me off.

When I sat down in math, the note waiting for me read, *So what happened?*

He said no. I wrote back. *I have to hike.*

The next morning we gathered in the lobby, loaded ourselves on the bus, and traveled to the Shenandoah Valley. The 62 of us were led by Mr. Whitzal with Mrs. Miranda, our Spanish teacher, following at the end with her daughter. I was mesmerized by the Shenandoah Valley. My Jewish camp in Malibu was a far cry from the peaceful forest we had been brought to. Part of the difference was the slightly orange and red tint of the leaves. I had gone to camp on the east coast occasionally, but always during the summer. This was mid-September. Some leaves change color in LA I suppose, but looking around I realized that I had never experienced proper autumn.

Preoccupied with my surroundings, I started to walk, relieved that the humidity had lessened. I walked slowly and took my time going down. As the trail got a little steeper and a lot rockier, I tried to keep my balance but I began tripping over uneven ground.

"Ow!" Rocks on the trail slammed me to the ground. Hard.

"Are you alright?" Janie and Stella were other members of the slow group.

"I don't know. My ankle really hurts," I sniffed, cradling my foot.

"Mrs. Miranda? I don't know if Natasha's okay," Janie called out.

Mrs. Miranda bent down to look at my ankle. It was already ballooning fast.

"Stella," she commanded, "Go tell Mr. Whitzal that Natasha's hurt her ankle, and that we're back here."

Stella glared at me and ran off. I could almost hear her say "spoiled brat." Using Janie and Mrs. Miranda as crutches, I picked myself up and attempted to limp down the trail. A few minutes later, Mr. Whitzal appeared from the woods.

"Yep. It's swelling. Try and keep off it. I told the group to wait at the fork in the road. We're not too far off. Mrs. Miranda, can you get her there? Good. I'll lead the group to the cabin and come back for you."

Mrs. Miranda, her daughter, Janie, and I hobbled down the hill until we came to a small clearing. Standing there were Stella, Mr. Whitzal, and about four other people.

"Where is everyone else?" Mrs. Miranda asked.

The panicked look on Mr. Whitzal's face told us everything we needed to know.

"I called after them," he shook his head. "I thought they heard me. They—well—I guess they didn't. I mean, I think they just they kept going."

"Kept going?" Mrs. Miranda repeated slowly. "You mean to say that there is a large pack of sixteen-year-old federal employees who are at this moment lost in the Shenandoah Valley?"

Mr. Whitzal stared back at her helplessly.

"We heard him and stopped. But everyone else kept going. I don't think they heard him," Stella explained.

"I'm sure we'll find them," I said encouragingly. "You said it was a downhill hike; how far could they have gone?"

Silence. Finally, Mr. Whitzal came to a decision.

"Okay, first we will get you all to the cabin. It's not far. Hopefully, we will find them along the way. They might have even gotten there already."

The group of five bored Interquest members sitting around in front of the cabin told us that this was not the case. Mr. Whitzal told them what happened, and they organized a search party amongst themselves. The rest of us sat down inside.

"It's a valley. They couldn't be far away," Mrs. Miranda offered with attempted optimism. Somehow she was no more convincing than I was. At this point it was 10 a.m.

Then it was 11.

12.

12:30.

At 1 pm, a van drove up. Two pages, Jack and Lennie, jumped out. Mrs. Miranda sprung to life. "They've been found!" she yelled.

"Well, we decided that the group was being kind of silly, so we decided to go off on our own," Jack explained sheepishly. "We found where our buses were parked. We were tired, so we took a nap. Then these men found us and brought us back here."

"Just the two of you?" I could see Mrs. Miranda's heart drop.

"Yep. Just the two of us."

Unfortunately, Mr. Whitzal reappeared at that moment.

"I heard on the radio they had been found," he exclaimed breathlessly.

"No, just these two have been found. These two. Two!" Mrs. Miranda held up two fingers for emphasis. She started breathing faster and pacing up and down the room. "We started with sixty-two. We now have ten people here. Ten! We have lost 52 pages in the Shenandoah Mountains! They have no water or food. It was supposed to be a short hike! One hour! It's almost two in the afternoon!" Mrs. Miranda was screaming now.

I stared at the ground as Mrs. Miranda demanded of no one in particular what she would tell the parents of 52 lost teenagers. It was my fault. No one had said that, but I knew it was. Stella would make sure I knew it. I would never live this down.

As if he could read my mind, Jack came over and whispered, "It's not your fault."

"It is, though."

"You told me that you tried to tell them about your ankle, right?"

"Yeah, but still…" my voice trailed off.

"See? Besides, I had fun. I got to know people that I never would have met otherwise. Who needs these silly Interquest people when you can get lost hiking for hours?" He smiled and nudged me. I laughed against my will.

"Come on," he said, "where's the food, I'm starving."

I got Jack and the others sandwiches. Mr. Whitzal called the park rangers, and a full-fledged search began.

3 o'clock.

4.

4:30.

5…

5:30.

And then they came.

They were hooting and hollering… all 52 of them. And they were holding apples. Each had at least 5 or 6.

They hugged each other, hugged the rangers who had found them, jumped up and down, and screamed. I felt a huge wave of relief, but by this point I was so embarrassed I couldn't be excited. I just smiled and hugged them, managing the occasional comment about how glad I was they were back. I wondered how many knew that it was my fault that they got lost in the first place. We loaded ourselves on the bus and waited for the teachers to take an excruciatingly accurate count.

I sat down next to Kelsey and across from Stella and Janie.

"You will not believe it!" Kelsey launched into the story. "We followed Achmed, you know, that guy over there, cause he said that he lived around here and knew the way, but we kept getting more and more lost! It was crazy, and no one had any water or anything!"

"Where did you get the apples?"

"That's the best part! We ended up at this farm and these people had heard that someone was looking for us so they gave us apples from their orchard. I was so hungry; I've already eaten about 3. I have so many. They gave us like 10 each!"

We got back to the dorm and piled into the elevator. Which of course then got stuck with all the weight (too many of us had jammed in). Someone handed me an apple. I turned around. It was Hani.

Twenty minutes later we were upstairs and I limped into my room. I threw the covers over my head. Stella hadn't spoken to me since we had arrived at the cabin, and I certainly didn't want to hear any of her comments now. I was humiliated enough. For the first time in my life, I really felt like the JAP that I had always joked I was.

Chapter 8: Two Princes

So what are you going to be for Halloween? I wrote to Hani during Math. Our notes had become my favorite part of the day. We sometimes gossiped about the other pages in the class.

Dean and I are going to be girls. Do you want to help? I need clothes and makeup and stuff. Dean's going to wear Whittany's stuff, he wrote.

Dean had begun dating a southern belle named Whittany. She was also from northern Florida—Jacksonville. She was a bit more down-to-earth than Brittany and suited Dean pretty well. He had gone through a few different girlfriends, and Hani had gotten increasingly jealous. Kelsey had been off with Ben quite a bit over the weeks that had passed. He sent her roses practically every day. She hung them up and dried them out. We had a collection of beautiful dried rose petals that Kelsey kept in a vase on her desk.

I wanted someone to send me roses every day. Heck, forget every day; once would have been nice. I wanted Hani to send me roses. Hani and I often talked about our respective roommates' relationships, comforting each other in our lack of social lives. I wanted to scream out that if he was really unhappy, he should date me. He would moan about not having a girlfriend, flirt with me endlessly, and then not make a move.

With Kelsey always off with Ben, Stella and I didn't see much of each other during the day. She was off with Janie, and I would hang out with Gretl or Dean and Hani. Whenever we were together, it was because she needed to show me how to do something. Our first few room inspections began with her yelling at me about not knowing how to vacuum, or clean a toilet, or mop the bathroom floor. She would spend half the time we spent together teaching me some domestic skill. I always thanked her, but she would just roll her eyes and say that she only did it so that I would stop being such a useless spoiled brat. Instead of taking offense, I constantly felt humbled. These were things I should have known, and was repeatedly annoyed at myself for my ignorance.

Other relationships were flourishing as Katrina and Gus had become a couple and many of the girls went to Arlington parties every weekend. Brittany had a succession of boyfriends. Hani and I joked about what they did at the parties. Sometimes we joked with Jack, who sat in front of us in Math. He fell asleep every single day.

Totally Jack is fragile, handle with care, Hani would write.

When he would start to tip over, Hani would stick a pen in his ear or something, and he would jolt up.

Sometimes Hani played with my hair. He made flowers and things with it, and he liked to imitate Mr. Anderson's moustache.

Mostly Hani and I passed notes. Lots and lots of notes. Sometimes we did math work. Mrs. Bowen gave so much partial credit, though, that as long as something was written on our paper we always managed to pull off a B.

I giggled at the idea of Dean and Hani dressed as girls. *Yeah.* I wrote, *I'd really like to see that.*

Do you have any clothes I can borrow? came the response.

Sure, I'll check and let you know later. You can try some stuff on.

What are you going to be? he wrote.

A hippie.

I'm down with that. You kinda look like one anyway.

I giggled, running my fingers through my long straight hair. *Thanks?* I wrote.

You can dress up like a guy and be our pimp tomorrow at the carnival, Hani suggested.

Kelsey's already dressing up like a guy, but I'd like to hang out with you two at the carnival anyway. I shrugged, trying to play it off.

I'd like that. He looked at me and smiled. I felt my face flush.

"Who wants to put the next problem up on the board? Hani? How about you?" Mrs. Bowen's voice interrupted. Jack jolted upright at the sound of her voice.

Hani reluctantly got up and walked to the blackboard. I turned back to my math homework.

That morning when we got to work, Mrs. Donnelly, the head of the Democratic pages, pulled me aside.

"Natasha, you know, each morning two pages are picked to open the doors to the house. This morning, it is your turn. I would suggest you rapidly tie your tie and make sure your shirt is tucked in."

"Wow, really? Am I going to be on C-span?"

"Of course. Now hurry and get ready."

I hastily readjusted my shirt as I raced over to a phone in the Cloakroom and called my parents. It was six in the morning in LA, but that didn't matter. I was going to be on TV!

"Hey, it's me, turn on C-span and hit record. I'm going to be opening the doors for the House this morning!"

My parents were confused (especially since I woke them up) but they recorded C-span as I, in my tied tie and tucked-in shirt, opened the door for that day's session. The rest of the day, I walked around feeling proud.

It was just starting to get dark when I left work that night, my spirits still high from my 15 seconds of fame. Shivering, I realized that it was getting too cold to wear only my blazer outside. I paused when I got to the corner. On one side was the annex, but on the other side was a park. I walked across the street to the park. It was beautiful. I'd never been so emotionally affected by nature before. Walking over, I felt the colored leaves beckoning in the sunset. The fountain in the middle of the park was on, the setting sun casting a shadow over the flickering water.

Seasons don't change in Los Angeles. Leaves don't change. How beautiful the world looked at that moment. There was something indescribable about the red, orange, and gold leaves that made everything just more… real. I closed my eyes and felt the softly blowing breeze on my face. I opened them to see if the colors were still there; as if one moment of darkness would steal this introduction to reality from me. The silhouettes of the trees with their changing leaves etched themselves into my consciousness. I wanted to take this sight back with me to LA.

"Natasha?" A voice behind me intruded into my moment. I spun around, surprised by the interruption. It was Kelsey.

"What are you doing?" she asked. "You look like you saw a ghost."

"I've never seen this before," I murmured.

"Seen what?" she asked confused.

"Fall. Autumn. I've never seen this. I've seen winter before, I mean, I've gone skiing and seen snow, but I've never seen the leaves change."

"And you hadn't noticed until now?"

"We spend all day inside. I mean, the tunnels and everything, I guess I just haven't been paying attention." To the leaves, as well as anything outside of myself.

Kelsey laughed. "True enough." From her tone I realized she understood both my meanings.

"Well, welcome to everywhere else in America that isn't Los Angeles," she continued. "What do you think of the real world?"

I thought for a moment. "It's amazing," I replied.

"You know," she paused, "they'll turn off the fountain soon."

"Why?" I asked.

"Well, it will get too cold. You know about winter, don't you? Water tends to freeze."

"That makes sense. It's just so different than where I come from. I wish they wouldn't. The fountain's so beautiful."

"They'll turn it back on when spring comes."

"I'll miss it in the meantime."

"I know, we all will. Well, now you've seen fall, congratulations. It's cold. Let's go inside."

We went to our room and I rummaged through the piles on the floor, looking for clothes to make Hani into a woman. Our room was a constant and complete disaster. Without my mother around to make sure I did not become a total slob, and living with Kelsey, who was also a total slob, the space between Kelsey's bed and mine was hazardous.

Stella's side somehow remained immaculate, but the only time Kelsey and I cleaned was for room inspection. We shoved our stuff under beds, in the closet, and on the empty top bunk. After we passed inspection, the clothes returned to their home on our floor.

I rooted through the mess and found a short skirt, stockings, and tight-fitting shirt to give to Hani. I grabbed some of my makeup and headed into the common room to get to work.

"Oh my G-d!" screeched Brittany, dressed fittingly as a sorority girl, when she walked into the lounge. "I could jus' eat you up, you are so adorable!" She ran over to admire Dean, who was really quite convincing as a woman. The tight skirt and black top we had dressed him in were really flattering, and his features lent themselves surprisingly well to a bit of lipstick and eye shadow. Hani was not so convincing. He had a bit too much of a 5'oclock shadow, and where as Dean was long and lean with a graceful body, Hani was a bit too pudgy to carry off stockings. No matter how much makeup we plied on him, he didn't look very feminine.

Kelsey looked pretty convincing as a guy- she was sporting the hip hop look and her short red hair was slicked back in a baseball cap. She even drew a moustache. Brittany and I took loads of pictures of her and Dean standing together in various silly poses. Hani scowled.

When we got to the carnival, Dean, Hani, and I went off on our own. Dean and I wanted to hang out with the larger group, but Hani wasn't really comfortable around them. He didn't like Brittany or Kelsey. He got along with Gretl, but she was off with Katrina and some of the others. We walked around, playing different games and going on some of the rides.

"Hey!" Dean yelled, whipping around.

"What happened?" I asked.

"Some guy just pinched my butt!" he moaned.

Hani and I couldn't stop laughing. We teased him about it all night. Guys kept coming up to Dean and asking him for his number. Hani joked that he should give it to them. By the end of the night, Dean decided he was never dressing up like a girl again.

Chapter 9: Wholesome

It was almost time for the election, which meant it was also almost time for the House to go out of session. Work was frantic. Many mornings we had shortened school hours because the House began its business before the usual 10 am. Then we would stay at work much later than the usual 5 pm. As the pressure to conclude business became more and more intense, our hours became longer. I still had yet to meet my own congressman, but I *had* gotten to meet Gopher from the "Love Boat." Otherwise known as Fred Grandy from Iowa. There was a rumor that Congressman Grandy had once been in an elevator with a page who had muttered, "Captain Stubbing needs you on the Lido deck." Legend had it that he had gotten so angry; he had the page kicked out. I was nervous about meeting him, but my parent's friend had worked with him on "Love Boat," and set up the meeting. I was careful not to mention his TV career when our photo was taken.

During the last weeks of the 102nd congress, work became even more frantic. President Bush had vetoed a bill to re-regulate cable companies. The House and Senate, both Democratic, sought to override the veto.

"What exactly is this bill?" I asked.

I was an overseer that week so I was one of the two pages who stayed on the house floor and answered calls for Pages. . Sitting at the desk next to Jack, I wondered what was going on. It was getting late and the House showed no sign of dismissal.

"I don't know. I just hope we get out of here soon. I'm hungry." He shrugged.

Mrs. Donnally came over to the group of us sitting by the page desk.

"Pages, the House will work late tonight, as will we. The cloakroom pages, the overseers, and the floor pages will remain. The rest have gone home." Her thick New England accent commanded our attention. She turned and walked back into the cloakroom.

The floor was busy. Most of the time, only a few congressmen gathered at any given time. Tonight, however, it seemed as though everyone had showed up.

Congressman Pickle from Texas came over to the page desk.

"Do y'all have the time?"

"It's 9:15," I answered.

He looked at me for a moment. "I said, do y'all have the time?" he repeated louder.

I had forgotten that he was almost deaf. "IT'S NINE FIFTEEN!" I yelled.

"Thank you kindly, little lady," he said, turning away.

"He forgot to put on his hearing aid again," Gretl sighed from the cloakroom door. "He's got his own special one here in the cloakroom, but sometimes he forgets to use it."

Congressman Taylor from Mississippi, otherwise known as the most gorgeous man in the world, had wandered over.

"Y'all don't happen to know when we're gonna get out of here, do ya?"

I shook my head.

"We have to still get past these amendments and then vote on the cable bill," Gretl responded. Apparently she had been paying more attention than I had.

"Well, I'm going to get myself a sandwich. See y'all shortly," he said.

"He's gone," Jack snickered, "you can wipe the drool from your chin now."

"He is perfection in human form," I cooed.

"Yeah," Gretl agreed. "He's so young. I think he's about 26. He always chats with us in the cloakroom. I guess since he's one of the youngest members, he likes talking to us because we are close to his age."

Jack rolled his eyes and sat back in his chair. I wondered where Hani had gone. He was a floor page, so I knew he was around.

Mrs. Donnally came back over. "Pages, will one of you take this run over to Senate Hart? I know overseers aren't supposed to leave the floor, but it's quieted down and it might be good to take a short walk."

A short walk? I thought, the Senate Hart office building was miles away. Gretl darted back into the cloakroom and Jack tried to look really busy.

"Natasha, do you mind?" she asked.

"Okay, I'll take it," I sighed.

I left the House floor and walked over to the Senate side. It had been a while since I had gone to that part of the building, so I took the wrong elevator and ended up by the old Supreme Court chamber. I wandered through the deserted hallways until I found stairs leading towards the basement. I weaved through the narrow passageways until I heard voices. Following the sound, I ended up on the landing right above the subways to the

Senate office buildings. An old man was propped between two large bodyguards. A few other people stood around them.

"Why hello there, darlin'," came the man's voice. I recognized him right away. Senator Strom Thurmond.

"Good evening, Senator," I said politely.

"So they're keeping you working, are they? Good. It's nice to know some things never change around here."

I didn't know what to say to that so I just smiled as I got into the subway car.

"Is there room for us all in this thing?" Senator Thurmond joked. Probably not, I thought, considering how many people seemed to be following him around. He talked and joked throughout the whole subway ride. I wondered how someone who could barely stand up on his own could be a senator. Strom Thurmond was famous for his filibuster against desegregation in the 1950's. He had held public office since the Great Depression, and I imagined that his belief systems had stagnated somewhere around World War II. Of course, after he died it emerged that he had fathered a child by an African American woman, but at the time, he was known around Washington as being vehemently racist. I stared at him across the subway car. His skin was like paper. He was tiny, frail, with a full head of hair that I figured was a really bad toupee.

I rushed off the train to finish my run and return to the page desk.

"It was crazy," I told Jack when I got back.

"The dude's got to be about 100 years old at this point, isn't he?"

"I don't know, but he had these two body guards who looked like they were actually holding him up. And there was a train of about 10 people following them."

"In case he fell and needed an ambulance?"

I laughed. "Probably. He was trying to joke with me, I think. He had his minders put him in the subway car with me."

"Oh yeah, each Senate building has its own little train, I forgot. Which one did you go to again?"

"Senate Hart. It's not a short ride either. He was trying to make jokes, and I was trying not to look like I was staring at him."

"Which you probably were," Jack pointed out, pushing back his long hair.

"Of course I was."

"Why do you think all his office pages are named after him?" Jack asked.

"I don't know. Maybe they're his illegitimate children or something." I shook my head. "Imagine. Being almost 100 and being a senator. Imagine all the stuff that has happened since he's been in office. Technology alone. I bet the underground subway trains weren't here in the 50's when he filibustered against desegregation."

Jack sighed and looked at his watch. "How long do you think we'll be here for?"

"I don't know, but this is fun. I've never seen the floor so busy," I answered, surveying the bustle of activity.

Jack paused and looked at me for a moment. "Hey," he said, suddenly serious, "What's going on between you and Hani?"

I was caught off guard. "What do you mean?"

"I mean, you guys spend a lot of time together. And you're always flirting during math class," he added, watching my reaction. As expected, I blushed.

"He's my friend."

"Really?" Jack looked at me skeptically.

"Yeah, come on, what's wrong with that?"

Jack shook his head. "Nothing. It's just that I heard that Hani likes Michelle and I see you spending so much time with him... I just don't want—I just wanted to know."

I felt like the wind had been knocked out of me. I was silent for a long moment. "No," I finally managed, "We're just friends."

Michelle was a Republican page. I looked to the other side of the floor, and sure enough, there was Hani talking to her.

"I wondered where he was," I accidentally said out loud. Jack gave me a look.

"We are just friends," I snapped.

"Are you telling me? Or yourself?"

"I..." The phone rang before I could respond. Jack answered.

"Democratic Page Service, how can I help you?" He shot me a look. "Yeah. Hi. Okay, I do. Any sandwich."

He turned to me. "It's your 'friend' Hani. He and Michelle are going to get food and he wants to know if we want anything."

My stomach hurt. "A sandwich is fine," I responded.

Trying to change the subject, I turned towards Mrs. Donnally, who was now standing by the page desk.

"Mrs. Donnally? How long have you worked here?"

"I've been head page for eight years. I've worked in politics for a long time, my dear. You know, I used to work for Sam Kennedy back in the day."

"Really?"

"He was a wonderful man. Wonderful family."

"Do you miss living in Massachusetts?" Jack asked.

"Now, pages, what kind of question is that? I love what I do. Always being right at the center of everything. There have always been pages here, you know. Since the beginning of Congress. You are part of a great tradition. And tonight you will be part of history," She said with a wink.

Congressmen continued to gather on the floor. Everyone's spirits were high. Finally, at 3 a.m., the House of Representatives overrode President Bush's veto on the cable bill. A huge cheer of joy rang from the Democratic side of the floor. I was so excited. I felt like I had somehow contributed to that moment, and I was proud of overriding the veto – even though I didn't know what the actual bill was about. At 6 in the morning, we were told to get breakfast. At 7 a.m., we were replaced by other pages who had actually been home and slept a bit. None of us felt tired. We were still too excited. Somehow I managed to sleep for a few hours. We were told to come back at 1 in the afternoon for concluding business. The House had finished; election season was upon us.

Chapter 10: Betty and Al

A few years back, Congressman Ackerman from New York had been in an elevator with two pages who were talking about bagels. He was dismayed when he realized that one of the pages had no idea what a bagel was. He decided to immediately rectify the situation, and established a tradition where once each semester, he had bagels, lox, and cream cheese flown in from his own deli in New York to feed the pages.

"How can a person not know what a bagel is?" I asked Kelsey, who was busy taking off her makeup after her date with Ben. Stella and Janie were gossiping on Stella's side of the room.

"I don't know. How could Brittany not know that a confederate flag is offensive? People here are kinda strange. The whole southern contingent calls any carbonated beverage 'Coke.' Have you noticed that?" She began imitating Brittany. "'What do you want to drink? A coke. What kind? 7 Up.' It's just strange."

"What do you call it?"

"Pop, of course."

"See, I would call it soda."

"Soda?"

"No, it would be cola," Stella chimed in.

"Soda pop," added Janie.

"How about we stick with carbonated beverage?" I laughed.

"That's so clinical," Kelsey said disapprovingly. "So, Natasha, did you see Hani and Michelle tonight? I think they are a proper couple."

I felt my face turn red again. "So?" I shrugged, trying to play it off. "He and I are just friends. Why should he not date Michelle?"

"Did you see them on election night?" Stella agreed. "They are definitely a couple."

The election had been an overwhelming success for the Democrats. Bill Clinton had won, and the Democrats had gained seats in the House and the Senate. Since most of the pages were Democrats, it had been a celebratory night. Only a handful of pages sat slumped in their chairs. Michelle was one of the very few Republicans in the room, but the majority of us were excited. We were having a party that Friday night to celebrate, after the bagel breakfast. We had the day off work.

One of the most important issues that came out of the election for us dealt with political labels. I learned that the difference between Conservatives and Liberals is not the same thing as the difference between Democrat and Republican. The Republicans who were socially liberal were quite different than the Democrats who were socially conservative. That term, most of the pages were socially liberal. In addition, pages such as Stella who had never met a Jew or Brittany who had sported her confederate flag were anxious to learn about new cultures. City people such as myself were mystified by those more rural backgrounds to which I had never had prior exposure. It was not so much about politics as it was about friendships. That was an exciting time, all of us learning to accept our differences.

We raced over to the Capitol for the bagel breakfast. It had been so long since I had eaten good lox.

I went to the table and began fixing myself a bagel. Sure enough, Lennie, from New Mexico, acknowledged that he did not know what a bagel was.

"How can you not know what a bagel is?" I asked.

"I've never had one." He shrugged.

"But haven't you heard of them?" I was baffled.

"Nope."

I turned towards the other side of the table where Brittany was standing, sporting a look of complete bewilderment.

"What's that?" asked Brittany, pointing to the lox, "Is it lobster?"

"Lobster? No. That's lox. It's smoked salmon," I replied.

"Ew. That's disgusting," she shrieked.

"It's good," I said, helping myself to another piece.

"Jew food," Hani interjected with a wink.

"Proper New York Jew food," I corrected with a smile.

"It looks weird, y'all," Brittany declared.

"Just try a piece," I urged.

She delicately helped herself to the smallest piece on the plate and took a tiny bite. Her brow furrowed.

"It's funny, but better than I thought it was gonna be."

"Here, put some cream cheese on the bagel and put some lox on top," I instructed.

She took a small bite. "Not bad. Enough of this food stuff, y'all are forgetting the important stuff. Natasha, you comin' to the party tonight?"

The food lesson was obviously over. "The one at the dorm? Yeah, of course."

"You're going to dance with me, right?" Hani asked.

"I'll think about it," I said, staring at him. He was looking at me intently.

"No, no, no," Brittany shook her head. "I mean the Arlington party."

"Oh, um, no. I think I'll just stay at the one in our building. Kelsey, are you going to the Arlington party?" I asked.

"No, Ben's out of town this weekend, so I'll stay and bond with you guys," she responded, her mouth full of bagel.

"Well, I'm gonna go out and have me some fun." Brittany turned and walked over to another group of girls to see if any of them would go with her.

I couldn't stop thinking about Hani. If he were really dating Michelle, why did he always flirt with me? We spent more and more time together, but when he talked about Michelle, it was always evasive. *Do you know Michelle likes me?* he would write. I would ask him if he liked her, and he'd say things like, *hmm... interesting.* Or, *She's cute.* And if I sat down without rubbing his neck he'd ask me, *what, no neck massage?* He kept me guessing about where I stood. And I didn't know what to say or how to talk to him about it.

"Don't think about it," came Kelsey's answer.

"Why? I really like him," I moaned when we got back to the room.

"I can't put my finger on it, but I can just tell that he's bad news."

"He's really sweet, though. And we get along really well."

"You get along well with Dean, too. And Jack. Seriously, do whatever you want, but that guy gives me bad vibes." She shook her head. Then she thought for a moment. "Natasha, have you ever had a real boyfriend before?"

I turned red with embarrassment. "Sort of. Mostly just at camp, though."

"Camp doesn't count. Everyone has boyfriends at camp. I mean, a serious, long-term relationship."

I shook my head. "No."

Kelsey sighed. "That explains it. You just want a boyfriend, and here's this guy who pays all kinds of attention to you. But it's the wrong kind, don't you see? He's after something. He knows you like him and he's taking advantage."

She came over and put her arm around me. "It will happen. Don't worry. You'll meet an awesome guy, fall in love, and it'll be great. Don't dwell on Hani."

"I try not to," I said quietly. "I don't know what my problem is."

She smiled. "We'll find you a man. Don't worry. Now, enough of this. We have work to do. It's our turn for clean up."

Before the dance, Kelsey, Stella, and I had clean up duty. Each week, one room was responsible for cleaning up after weekend dinners. During the week we ate at the Capitol Hill cafeterias, but on Saturday and Sunday, food was brought in. This particular Saturday, the meal had involved potato salad.

"Hey, Natasha, can you wash out the potato salad vat?" Kelsey asked. I had been throwing away paper plates.

"I don't know if she knows how," Stella chirped.

"I can clean out a vat of potato salad," I defended. I was sick of Stella always making me feel like less of a person. Come on, I could do the simple task of cleaning one container. I picked up the vat, dumped most of the remaining potato salad in the trash, and marched into the common room bathroom to wash the container out in the sink. It was too big, so I decided to use the bathtub instead. I put the vat into the bathtub and turned on the water. I got a sponge and started scrubbing the inside, alternating scrubbing, dumping, and rinsing. The large container looked pretty clean. I was about to proudly declare my success when I noticed that the water level in the bathtub continued to rise instead of circling down the drain.

"Something's wrong," I said nervously after a few minutes of watching the dirty water rise.

"Huh? Just wash it out," Kelsey called from the other room.

"No, I mean, the water. The bathtub's filling up, I can't get it to go down the drain."

Stella stomped into the bathroom. "Did you get all the potato salad out before you rinsed the container?"

"I thought I got most of it. The rest would just go down the drain, wouldn't it?"

"This isn't a kitchen! There's no garbage disposal!" Stella yelled. I watched in dismay, frozen in place as the potato salad water began streaming out of the bathtub.

"Don't just stand there, get some paper towels. Quickly!" Stella took control, turning off the water, which, in my wide-eyed horror, I had neglected.

"Here are some garbage bags! Try and scoop some of it into these!" Kelsey thrust the garbage bags into my hands. I tried to push the yellow watery goop into the bags with my hands, but it just seemed to spread the mess around.

"What's going on here?" Maya, the proctor, had come to see how we were doing. She immediately saw the murky water, which, although Stella had turned off the water, had flooded the bathroom and had started to seep into the common room carpet.

"What on earth?" She stared in disbelief.

All my insecurities boiled to the surface. Stella was right all along. I was a useless, naïve, sheltered spoiled brat. I couldn't do this one simple thing. I couldn't do anything right. Tears welled up and spilled over as I tried in vain to mop up the water. "I'm so sorry, I didn't think. I'm really, really sorry. I'll clean it up, I promise." The more I tried to clean it up, the more of a mess I made. I tried to stop crying and pull myself together, but that just made me more upset. Hiccupping, gulping down my tears, covered with potato salad water and paper towels, I collapsed to the ground, repeating, "I'm so, so sorry. You're right. I am useless, I can't do anything. I can't clean anything, I'm hopeless."

Stella stood over me with paper towels, a mop, and a look of mingled exasperation and irritation. As she looked down at me, a heap of potato salad and tears, all of a sudden her face dissolved into a grin as a huge burst of laughter came out of her. She laughed so hard and for so long that she had to lean on the mop for support. After a few minutes, she got up and came over to give me a hug. I sobbed into her shoulder. "I'm so stupid."

Stella let me cry for a few minutes. Once I had calmed down, she said, "Well, Natasha, the JAP from Los Angeles, how about I show you how to clean it up, and we go from there?"

"But I'm such an idiot."

"No, not an idiot. Just, you have a lot to learn about some relatively basic things. Come on, we got you through Laundry 101, didn't we?"

She handed me a dry paper towel, and together we cleaned up the potato salad mess.

Something about that moment filled in the chasm that had separated Stella and the things I knew and the things she knew were so different. We had understood that, but neither of us had really appreciated it.

I was relieved when we finally finished cleaning and began to get ready for the dance. I lent Stella some of my clothes and showed her the proper way to apply mascara.

We spent most of that night dancing in one big group. Brittany and her friends had already left to go to the Arlington party. Hani stayed on the sidelines as Jack, Gretl, and I jumped around. Dean was off in a corner with Whittany. I kept waiting for Hani to come dance with us, but he just stood off to the side. Michelle stayed on the other side of the room talking to some of the other Republican pages. I kept looking over, hoping that Hani would ask me to dance. He never did. Kelsey informed me that if I asked Hani to dance, she would go into our room, lock the door, and throw my clothes out the window. Jack refused to let me feel sorry for myself, grabbing my hands and dancing in the most ridiculous manner possible, whipping his long hair at me. After a while, I stopped looking in Hani's direction and let myself have fun.

None of us noticed when Brittany's group came home from their party. I didn't even notice when the proctors all suddenly left the room at the same time. And I didn't realize, until I saw one of the girls lying precariously on the floor by her room, that any of them were drunk.

Chapter 11: Unpagely

"Excuse me, my dear, may I have a word with you?" The school guidance counselor, Mrs. Caulfield, tapped me on the shoulder.

"Yes?" I wondered what she wanted.

"Well, I can't help but noticing, my dear, you need to tuck in your shirt and tie your tie in the mornings. You haven't looked very... pagely. Is everything alright?"

Pagely? I thought. What the hell does that mean? I looked at her for a moment, wondering if she was serious. Her eyes, a mixture of concern and disapproval, convinced me that she was, so I apologized and began tying my tie.

"I'm not much of a morning person," I explained.

"Yes dear, but you are a federal employee. I know you are from Los Angeles, and I'm sure they do things... differently over there. But, my dear, you have a responsibility to yourself and to the United States Government. Be proud. You will never be able to handle college if you cannot take care of yourself." The saccharine, condescending tone of voice was not enough to convince me that success in college was remotely linked to a tucked- in shirt. Nor did I understand how my hometown tied into anything. However, I obeyed.

"That's better. Now, if there is anything bothering you, be sure to let me know and we can work through it. A tidy page is a happy page." She patted me on the head as if I were a puppy dog and walked away.

I stared after her in disbelief for a moment and then headed to math class. I slouched down in my seat and waited for Hani to appear.

Mrs. Caulfield's psycho. I wrote to Hani. *Ever since those girls were given restriction for getting drunk, they have been freaking out over everything.*

Hani nodded and rolled his eyes. *Tell me about it,* he wrote back.

Can you imagine? Seven weeks of restriction. They have to be in their rooms by seven every night! I shook my head.

I'm can't believe Brittany didn't get restriction. I don't know what she said that got her out of it. How many of them are in trouble?

I think 5. That other girl, Erika, was in a really sorry state when I saw her, came my response.

Brittany and some of the other girls had gone to the Arlington party and had come back completely drunk. The party in our building meant that every proctor we had was on duty. The girls didn't seem to remember that. Erika, especially, had barely been able to stand up straight. They had spent the whole weekend being interrogated by the proctors, who then gave most of them seven weeks restriction. Brittany had somehow escaped punishment. I did not understand how that was possible, but not having been involved in the incident, I didn't feel it was my place to ask. Restriction meant that you could not leave your room after 7 p.m. every night. We had no computers in our rooms, and televisions were only in the common rooms. Locked in after 7 p.m. seemed like a recipe for complete boredom, at least to me.

"Now pages, you will have a test next Wednesday on chapters 10 and 11. Don't forget to show your work." Mrs. Bowen's voice interrupted our note-passing for a moment. "You may spend the rest of the period working on your homework so you can enjoy tomorrow's WISP without fretting."

Hani slumped in his chair. *This is dumb. This class is too easy, and I do not want to take that field trip tomorrow.*

I nodded. I thought about the dance. He hadn't asked me to dance, but he hadn't been with Michelle either. I wanted to ask him the question. It had been pressing on my mind for too long. Finally, I gathered up my courage. *Are you dating Michelle? Please tell me. I keep hearing that you are, but you never talk about it.* My hand shook as I wrote the note and passed it over to him.

He laughed out loud, causing Mrs. Bowen to smile and say, "See, I told you Math was your favorite subject."

Hani snickered and worked intently—pleasing Mrs. Bowen. However, he was working on a note that said, *Do you know Michelle likes me?*

Yeah, you keep saying that, but that wasn't the question. I raised an eyebrow.

She wants me. She's cute too. But so are you. He winked when he handed that note to me.

I blushed. The bell rang. Gathering my books, I asked, "So that's a no?"

Hani winked again and headed out of the room.

The next day, our WISP took us to the capital of Virginia—Richmond. I sat by the window and stared outside. Nearly all the trees were barren. The empty branches swirled around empty fields. It seemed so lonely. As if they were reaching out, longing for their lost foliage. Across the bus, Hani was sitting next to Michelle. I looked back at the dying landscape, commiserating with the loss. In spring, the trees would grow again. I wondered if I would too. The flowers would rise... and apparently so would the south. I stared at Brittany's ample chest, which was covered by a sweatshirt that said, "Save up your confederate money, boys, the south will rise again."

I gaped in disbelief at her top. "Where did you get that?" I asked in astonishment.

"What, this little ole thing? My daddy gave it to me. It's perfect for this trip, isn't it? Ooh, this is just so exciting!" She was practically jumping up and down. Jack came over to me and shook his head.

"Do you believe her?" he said, disapproving.

"She's actually nice. She doesn't mean anything by it, I don't think."

"Yeah, well, the best thing about her is her boobs." I looked at him in disgust. "Don't look at me like that, it's true. Even you have to admit that she has the biggest hooters in the whole page program. I bet she's just wearing that sweatshirt to make people like me look."

"I think she's wearing that sweatshirt because she is living in a pre-civil war part of *Gone with the Wind*."

"Well, at least this is the last trip before break. Are you going home for Thanksgiving?" he asked.

"No, it's too far. I'm going to visit my grandmother in Vermont. What about you?

"Yeah, I'm going home. I leave Tuesday."

"Welcome to the capi'tl of Verginia." The tour guide's thick southern accent interrupted. "If y'all will follow me, we will begin bay looking at this luvely statue of the wonderful Gen'ral Robert E. Lee."

"Don't ya just love the south?" Jack's high-pitched mocking whisper said into my ear, "y'all come back now, ya hear!"

I couldn't help laughing.

"Y'all be quiet. This is a solemn moment!" Brittany's whisper didn't seem different from her usual screech, but we followed quietly all the same.

Chapter 12: I Swear

Thanksgiving break felt far too short. I traveled up to Burlington, Vermont to see my grandmother. It was so cold up north that it almost made DC feel warm. My grandmother bought me a winter coat and instructed me in the correct use of scarves, gloves, and hats. Los Angeles never required an understanding of winter accessories. I dreaded going home to 72-degree weather at Christmas time and then having to come back to real live winter. Everyone had said that DC's winter was mild. I didn't know what that meant as I had been freezing. Of course, once I entered the Capital building I had to shed external layers, as the heating was so strong, I would broil.

There were parts of the Capitol that were climatically strange. There was a strong wind that practically knocked you down when you entered the Capitol from the tunnel that led to the Cannon office building. It seemed to come from nowhere. There were no doors or windows, as the entire tunnel system was underground. This tunnel let you out in the Capitol's basement, parts of which were freezing, parts of which were saunas. Since the house was out of session, we spent more time in school and found ourselves doing less runs. We all hung out in the cloakrooms, which were freezing.

The first day back from Thanksgiving break, we were told to keep our coats with us for history class. Mr. Whitzal walked our class outside and down to the end of the block. We stood outside shivering in the rushing wind as he spoke.

"This building," he yelled, pointing at an old brick structure on the corner, "is where the Americans first saw the British army before they burned down most of the Capitol and the White House during the War of 1812. Any questions?"

We all shook our heads.

"Good. Now, let's go back inside. We will proceed by discussing the after-effects of the war," he concluded.

"So that was the War of 1812." Hani walked next to me.

"You know," I looked at him, "I'm supposed to take the U.S. history AP exam at the end of this year."

He laughed. "Yeah, you're screwed."

"Thanks. Way to make me feel better."

"No problem. Anytime. And don't you love having longer classes?" He rolled his eyes.

"I so don't like having longer school days. I wish the House would get back into session so we could finish at 10 again. I don't understand why they make the class times longer but we still have to start so early," I complained.

"Who knows? At least we have another break soon. Christmas, then the inauguration, then the fall pages are outta here."

He seemed happy about that. I couldn't understand how he could be happy about it. I didn't like the thought. I had tried to forget that most of my closest friends were only there for one semester. Kelsey and Jack would leave after the inauguration. There would be

40 new people showing up to replace them. I knew that Stella, Janie, Hani, Dean, and Gretl, would still be around, which was comforting, but Michelle was also here for the year. She was a republican page–and ultra conservative in her views. I was fast developing a hatred for her - and we had barely ever spoken. How can he date someone so conservative? I thought. My thoughts turned back to Kelsey's imminent departure.

"I'm really sad about that. I don't want Kelsey to leave."

"Don't get sad. I'll still be here." He put his arm around me. I felt my whole body melt into the sidewalk.

"I know. I'm glad." I managed.

That night Hani called my room. Kelsey answered, thinking it was Ben. Her face fell as she thrust the phone at me.

"It's your socially challenged boyfriend."

"Thanks," I said as I tripped over the pile of clothes in front of the phone. Kelsey snickered.

"Hello?"

"Hi, Nat, it's Han."

"So I'm Nat now?"

"It's easier. Less syllables."

"Ha-ha. Okay, so Han. What's going on?"

"Nothing much. Dean snuck upstairs to hang out with Whittany, and I wanted to talk to you."

"How did he manage to do that? The doors are alarmed."

"I don't know. He and Lennie figured something out so they could see Whittany and Tina. What are you up to?"

"Not much. Janie and Stella are doing some homework, Kelsey was waiting for Ben to call, and I was just sort of milling about."

"Did I already ask you if you are going home for Christmas? You didn't go home for Thanksgiving, right?"

"Yeah, but I am going to LA for this break. And it's Hanukkah for me, don't forget."

"That's right. Mini United Nations. Will you call me from LA?" My heart began to beat faster. I tried to play it cool.

"Maybe, if I feel like it."

"Thanks, Nat. Well, I'll let you sleep I guess. See you in class tomorrow?"

"Yeah, see you then."

I hung up the phone and looked over at Kelsey. "I did ask him about Michelle before. He never really answered me."

She looked concerned, "Be careful, Natasha. I don't like what he's doing. I know Michelle thinks they are a proper couple."

"He never told me that. Why would he call me if he was dating her?"

"I don't know, but I hope for your sake that Michelle's wrong."

"Well, we are just friends. I mean, nothing's happened or anything."

"You should really keep it that way."

I lay down on my bed and stared at the ceiling. "Kelsey, what am I going to do when you leave?"

"You'll be fine. That is, so as long as you take my advice, find a real man and stay away from Hani.

Anyway, it's not for a while, and we have the inauguration to look forward to. I wonder if we'll get to meet any stars. Did you know that there are all these famous people coming? Barbara Streisand is singing at the ball! And Maya Angelou's speaking!"

"You are so lucky to work in Ways and Means. Don't you get to sit onstage or something?"

"Yeah, don't you?"

"No. I just get a ticket to stand out in the cold with everyone else."

"Hey, you'll have fun anyway. Maybe Hani will be your date to the ball," she added sarcastically.

I sighed and pulled the covers over my eyes.

Chapter 13: Bagels, Oranges, and Galas

While Thanksgiving had felt too short, Christmas was far too long. I missed Kelsey and Stella. I especially missed Hani. Jack called me a few times while I was home, but Hani didn't. I wondered if he called Michelle. I thought about calling him, but I didn't know what I would say. I lay in bed dreaming that he would dump Michelle and profess his love for me. Knowing how ridiculous that thought was, the best thing to do was to attempt to ignore my feelings and let myself appreciate being home with my family. The plane ride back to DC was nerve-wracking. Had he thought about me at all? Why hadn't he called?

I raced up to my room as soon as I got to the building. Kelsey was lying on her bed moaning.

"Hey there!" I yelled, "How was your break?" I had planned on dropping my stuff in my room and searching for Hani, but Kelsey's reaction stopped me from leaving.

"I have mono," was the muffled response.

"What? I couldn't hear you."

"She has mono," Stella explained from the other side of the room. "She's been lying there all morning. Her doctor told her to wait to come back but she decided to ignore him."

"I'm fine," Kelsey whimpered. "Do you smell something funny?"

"No," I replied, "I just talked to you last week, when did you get sick? And isn't mono really contagious?"

"It hit me a few days ago, but I don't think I'm contagious any more. Something smells." She turned over in bed, burying her head in her pillow.

"Whatever," Stella rolled her eyes. "Natasha, are y'in hungry? Janie and I are gonna get food."

"Sure, I'll come along," I replied. I would find Hani later.

We went to a restaurant on Pennsylvania Avenue called Pete's. No sooner had we walked in when a waitress rushed up to us.

"You sit down. You want cheeseburger? Three cheeseburger. Yes. Fries. Yes. Drink. Okay."

We sat.

"Did we just order?" I asked.

"I think so, I hope you like cheeseburgers," Stella laughed.

"So how were your breaks?" I asked.

"Mine was good, restful," Janie replied.

"I worked. Same ole job, cleaning service in the mall." Stella answered.

"You worked as a cleaner in a mall?" I looked at her strangely.

"Yeah, it's good money. And we didn't get paid during break, so I needed to do something."

Pages made about 12,000 dollars over the year. I thought that was awesome. My parents pointed out that that was how much my private school tuition in LA was per year. Stella pointed out that most people in this world couldn't afford private school tuition. One of the funniest things about our salaries was the fact that we each paid tax from our respective state. Even though we each technically were paid the same amount, my being from California versus Stella from West Virginia meant that she pocketed $200.00 more per month than I did- simply because she paid less tax.

My eyes drifted towards the window. I saw Hani, Dean, Michelle, and Whittany walking past Pete's towards the main street. I felt my stomach climb into my throat. Looking away quickly, I tried to change the subject.

"So, should we be worried about the fact that Kelsey has mono?" I asked.

"You're the one whose stuff shares the floor with her stuff," Stella pointed out. "Half the time you wear each other's clothes."

"That's true," I acknowledged. Most of the time I would pick up whatever item of clothing was closest to me. And half of the time that item of clothing was Kelsey's. She did the same thing so we didn't worry about it.

"I didn't smell anything, though." I pointed out.

"Neither did I. I think she's just delirious," Janie added.

"Cheeseburger, fries, drink." The waitress dumped our food in front of us.

"Thank you?" I said, slightly confused.

"So, have you heard? We are going to the Presidential Gala," Janie squealed.

"The rehearsal for the Presidential Gala," Stella corrected.

"It doesn't matter, Fleetwood Mac is performing, and Barbara Streisand, and everything. It's going to be amazing!" Janie refused to allow Stella to dampen her spirits.

"Hey you guys!" Gretl came into Pete's with Jack. They sat down at our table.

"Hi there, how was your break?" I asked.

"Cold. I'm glad to be back."

"Same here," agreed Jack. "Did we just order food when we came in?"

I laughed. "Yes. We did too. This place is nuts."

"Guess what! I was picked to work the inauguration!" Gretl announced.

"Really? You are so lucky, how did that happen?" I asked.

"They just picked people at random. Kelsey's supposed to work too, isn't she? Because she works for Ways and Means?"

"Yeah, but she has mono. I don't know if she'll be able to," I pointed out.

"She has mono?" Jack asked.

"Yeah. She says our room smells," Stella piped in.

"Poor girl. I hope she feels better," Gretl said with a mouth full of my fries.

Kelsey didn't feel better that night. Or the next night. Two mornings later we caught her practically sleepwalking to school wearing white sweats with her gray skirt and blazer. She kept complaining over and over again about our room smelling. We tried to be comforting, but she would just mope and wander around. She complained about feeling tired, sick, and sweating through all her blankets. We brought her food, but she said the smell was too strong in our room for her to eat anything. We all figured she was delirious. However, a week later, I smelled something funny.

"Okay, now I smell it." I announced the second I walked through the door. Stella was behind me, and sniffed at the air.

"Yeah, what is that?" she said. "That's awful."

"I tooooolllllddd you! Make it stop!" whined a drugged up Kelsey. Stella and I sniffed around until we located the direction of the stench.

"I think it's coming from this crate," I sniffed.

"Yeah, what's in here?" Stella and I dug around in the crate until we discovered the source of the smell. Stella gingerly lifted up a foul-smelling bag of fuzzy white mold mixed with brown and orange mush.

"Rotten bagels and oranges? What are these from?"

"Oh, I was looking for those!" Kelsey exclaimed. "My mom sent them last month but I couldn't find them before I left."

We stared at her for a moment, and then all of us burst out laughing.

Stella, Kelsey and I spent the rest of the night chatting about the upcoming events. Kelsey's health seemed to improve upon removal of the rotten foods. Ben had sent her extra bouquets of roses, with notes gushing about how much he missed her and that he couldn't wait for her to be well enough to see him. He was so sweet, and I wished that I could meet someone who would treat me as wonderfully. With only a few weeks left in the semester, Kelsey knew that she would have to make some decisions about her relationship. She was going back to Michigan, and Ben lived in Virginia. I admired how rational she was about the whole thing. She loved him, but also knew that long distance relationships were hard. They would both be going off to college, living different lives, and growing in different directions. She was determined to enjoy their last weeks together while not allowing herself any delusions regarding their future.

Stella and I listened to her, admiring her honesty. We both were staying in Washington, yet neither of us had local boyfriends who showered us with flowers. There was something seemingly unfair in that irony, yet Kelsey held no animosity towards us. She accepted what was true. I wished I could do the same with Hani. I wanted to put him out of my mind and accept the fact that he didn't think of me as more than a friend. Somehow, that was much easier said than done. He had barely spoken to me since we got back from break. I had looked for him when we had gotten back from Pete's. He had been sitting in the common room, snuggling with Michelle. I had pretended that I was looking for something else and raced back to my room. He slept during most of math class so our note-writing had reached a standstill. I tried to ignore how upset that made me and devoted my focus to the inauguration festivities and the limited time I had left with Jack and Kelsey.

a run sheet

My First restriction slip

It was a day of infamy.
A night of friendship.
And the end of innocence.

U.S. House of Representatives
Page School

ROOM LJ-A12, LIBRARY OF CONGRESS
WASHINGTON, DC 20540-9996

PHONE (202) 225-9000

OFFICIAL TRANSCRIPT

SCHOOL YEAR 1992-1993

STUDENT _____ WALLACE, NAOMI _____

First Semester SUBJECT	INSTRUCTOR	1st Qtr	2nd Qtr	Term Exam	Term Grade	Honors Course	Second Semester SUBJECT	INSTRUCTOR	3rd Qtr	4th Qtr	Term Exam	Term Grade	Honors Course
U.S. History	Mr. Weitzel	86	94	87	94								
American Lit.	Dr. Mawer	89	89	73	87								
Alg.II/Trig.	Ms. Bowen	85	86	83	85								
Advd.Spanish	Mrs.Miranda	92	92	84	91								
Work Experience	Dr. Knautz	94	93		93		Work Experience						
WISP	Dr. Knautz	92	88		90		WISP						

45	48	Days Enrolled
5		Excused Absences
		Unexcused Absences
	1	Tardies

TEACHERS' COMMENTS:

Fall Semester—
First Quarter   *Naomi's background in Spanish is strong, but her effort is erratic. Sra. Miranda*

Second Quarter   *Neatness counts! Sra.*

Spring Semester—
Third Quarter

Fourth Quarter

Standardized Test Scores

STUDENT NAME		YEAR	GRADE	VERBAL	VERBAL %ILE	MATH	MATH %ILE	SELECTION INDEX	SEL.IND %ILE	OPTION CODE
WALLACE NAOMI	C	92	JR	46	68	46	52	138	65	

Accredited by the Middle States Association of Colleges and Schools. One-half Carnegie Unit per s
Classes meet for forty-five minutes five times weekly.

94

U.S. Congressional Page
Winter Formal
January 16, 1993

me & a Dallas Cowboy.

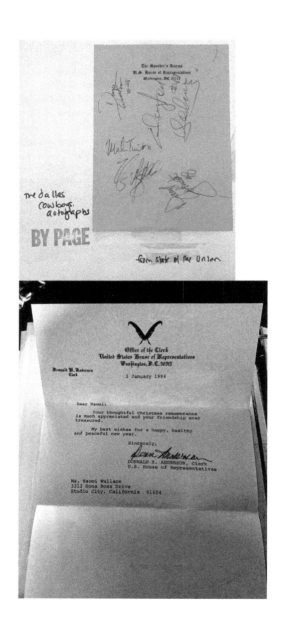

The Speaker's Rooms
U.S. House of Representatives
Washington, DC 20515

[autographs]

The dallas
cowboys.
autographs

BY PAGE

from State of the Union

Office of the Clerk
United States House of Representatives
Washington, D.C. 20515

Donald K. Anderson
Clerk   3 January 1994

Dear Naomi:

        Your thoughtful Christmas remembrance
is much appreciated and your friendship ever
treasured.

        My best wishes for a happy, healthy
and peaceful new year.

                Sincerely,

                [signature]
                DONALD K. ANDERSON, Clerk
                U.S. House of Representatives

Ms. Naomi Wallace
3312 Dona Rosa Drive
Studio City, California 91604

100

Chapter 14: House Pages Can Survive

"Hey, Natasha, I want to show you something!" Jack chased after me as I headed towards the Senate side on a run.

"What's up?" I asked.

"Well, have you been down into the catacombs?"

"The what?"

"You know, when dead people's coffins are put in the middle of the capitol building so that people can pay their respects. They lay in state. Dead presidents and such. They lie on this thing, a catafalque. It's this big, black, coffin holder thing. They keep it in the catacombs. Do you want to see?" he asked.

"Yeah, that sounds awesome!" I was excited. Inauguration fever had taken over the capital. Kelsey was feeling better, and I knew she would probably be able to work. Meanwhile, the rest of us were trying to take advantage of the last few weeks we had before the fall pages left. Jack led me downstairs to the first floor of the Capitol, under the Rotunda. From there we went down a flight of stairs that was off to the side near the Capitol chapel. Ending up by the back entrance, we turned, moving under the stairs into a tunnel. There, gated off, was a black bed-looking platform, the perfect size for a coffin. There was a plaque with a list of names on the wall next to it – all the people laid in state. Underneath the list was the word, Catafalque.

"This is what people are laid in state are placed on," Jack announced proudly.

"Wow," was all I could say at first. Jack and I stood next to each other, looking around.

After staring for a few minutes, I shivered. "It's really spooky down here."

"I know." He put his arm around me protectively. "It's kinda cool though."

"How long have you known about this?" I asked.

"For a while. I wanted to show you though." Jack turned to look me in the eyes. "You've been a good friend, Natasha. I'll miss you when I leave."

I smiled and gave him a hug. "I'll miss you too. You better come to visit me."

"I will," he said. "I promise."

Jack and I stayed down in the catacombs for a while, looking around and exploring the different tunnels. This secret world seemed so different from even the tunnels that we traveled through daily. The air was thick with memories, a living testament to the two hundred years of politics that frolicked in the stones above and below this hidden cavern. The catafalque provided a centerpiece; a final resting place for those whose lives were dedicated to the perseverance of this building and all it stood for. This labyrinth, drenched in history, existed in our minds to remind us that we were a part of it. We were not immune to the power of the hidden passageways, nor would we allow ourselves to forget the moment in which that power filled our consciousness.

The inauguration seemed to harness that power and give it life outside the Capitol... outside Washington. The Mall pulsated with energy. Standing in the crowd, watching Clinton take office, I was proud to be part - however small - of Congress. When I look back, I remember that moment. I was proud of my country, and proud to be an American. Like the catafalque below the rotunda, pages exist below the surface of the political machine. I stood in the cold knowing that when everyone around me left, I would be going back to work in the centerpiece of the inaugural ceremony.

Kelsey was much better by the inauguration. She got to work onstage with the other few lucky ones who were chosen, while I stood in the cold with everyone else. My family came for the inauguration, although my brother wasn't feeling well. His leg hurt and he was hobbling around the whole time. My father managed to make an appointment for me to finally meet my congressman. I got my picture taken with him, although he didn't seem to really know who I was. I wished that my Member would host bagel breakfasts or take me out to lunch, but at least I got to meet him.

We all attended the rehearsal for the presidential gala, complete with Fleetwood Mac and Barbara Streisand. Stars attending the inauguration festivities, such as Chevy Chase, came to the House floor to look around. However, then the end of January crept up on us; it was time for the fall pages to go home.

I was never someone who allowed myself to cry. The potato salad incident had been the only time that year when I wept, and that was in response to my own stupidity. Knowing that my best friends were leaving, however, forced a sense of emptiness upon me that I was unable to manage or understand. I knew they felt the same way. Kelsey put on a brave face, but she was crying softly as she began the cleaning-up process.

I sat in my room and watched Kelsey pack.

"Is this yours or mine?" she sniffed, holding up a sweatshirt.

"Take it if you want it, I don't remember whose it is."

"You're not being very helpful."

"What's going to happen when you leave?"

"You still have Hani," she said sarcastically.

"Ha-ha. Thanks. Seriously, he hasn't called me or anything. I've barely even talked to him since break was over." That was true. He hadn't even really passed me any notes in math class for a while. I didn't know what to do, and I was so upset about everyone leaving, I didn't want to make the sadness worse by thinking about him.

"It's better that way. He's with Michelle. I think you need to get over him and move on. Listen," she said, sitting down at the end of my bed, "I'm just a phone call away. And I'll come to visit in the spring. Stella's still here, and Janie. It'll be fine. I promise."

"I know." I attempted a smile. "We still have a few days anyway, I don't know why I'm getting all upset now."

"Hey you guys!" Gretl burst into the room. "Have you heard?"

"Heard what?" I asked.

"Brittany's been kicked out of the page program!"

"Kicked out? We're leaving this week as it is!" Kelsey's eyes grew big with disbelief.

"What did she do?" I asked.

"Alcohol or drugs or something. She was caught coming in last night. They called her congressman and everything. She's being sent home today!" Gretl rushed to the next room to pass on the news. Kelsey and I stared wide-eyed at each other before running to Brittany's room.

"I jus can't believe those proctors. How dare they!" She was frantically packing.

"What happened?" I asked.

"I jus' went out and had a little fun, and when I got back y'all'd think that I was some kinda felon or something. I'm madder than a sheep at shearing time. They're jus' all against me." She threw her "confederate money" sweatshirt into her suitcase.

"I'm so sorry, Brittany," I said.

"I'm sorry for you. You have ta live with these proctors for a whole nother semester. I'm gonna go home to my daddy's house, and have myself some fun."

"Ms. Witt?" Julie, the assistant proctor was standing at the door. "It's time."

"I'm comin', I'm comin'. You ladies have yourselves some fun this week, d'ya hear?" With that she gave us all hugs, picked up her luggage, and walked out.

"Do you think we'll ever see her again?" I asked Kelsey.

"Who knows? Probably not." We stood in silence for a few minutes, letting her off-the-cuff answer resonate. Probably not. Probably never.

"Come on," Kelsey continued, shaking off the truth of the moment. "We have that prom thing tonight. We better get ready."

Prom was a bittersweet event. I spent most of the night dancing with everyone in a big group. Then suddenly, Hani came up to me. "End of the Road" was playing.

"This is our song. Wanna dance?"

"I didn't know we had a song," I croaked.

"Of course we do." He smiled and took my hand.

He began to sing along, "So now we've come, to the end of the road, and we can't let go."

I put my head in his shoulder, feeling his arms tighten around me. He would be staying. This was not the end for us, but it was the end for so many others.

Kelsey, Jack, and the rest of the fall pages left a few days later. When Jack came in to say goodbye, I began to sob.

"It's okay, we'll see each other soon. I'm going to come to visit in the spring. I already made the reservations," Jack soothed, rubbing my back.

"Really?" I choked.

"Yes. I promise," he said, "and I'll call you and you call me, okay?"

"I will. I promise too." I gave him a huge hug. He smiled again and headed out the door. In the spring, I thought. When things start growing again.

Kelsey's parents came to get her a few moments later. I couldn't stop crying. Neither could Stella or Janie.

"Call all the time, promise?" I managed through my tears.

"I will. And you call me. It's okay; don't let it get to you. I'm just grateful I got to come here. I won't forget you. I promise. Hey, you guys, hey, remember, you'll be great. All of you. And I'll see you soon." She gave each of us a hug as her parents lugged her suitcases down to their car.

"I'll see you all in page heaven!" she yelled as she left.

For a long while there was silence. Despite my clothes still strewn across the floor, our room felt empty. My stuff alone was not enough to close up the vacancy that was left by Kelsey's departure. Stella, Janie, and I sat and stared at Kelsey's empty bed when there was a knock at our door.

"Girls?" It was Julie. "Remember, the new pages will be coming tomorrow? Well, there will be some changes. Stella? I'm going to ask for you to move down the hall. It's only right that you split up to allow yourselves the opportunity to meet as many new people as possible. Oh, and Natasha. Your new roommate's trunk is here. I'm just going to put it against this wall." She brought in a huge trunk that read, "ANNIE" on the front. Stella followed Julie out the door to find out where she was moving.

I needed to get out. I grabbed my coat, fled the room, and ran across the street to the park. The fountain had been turned off for the winter, leaving the stone structure barren in the center. I climbed into the fountain and settled in one of the curved arms. There, in the cold, I sobbed.

"Natasha? Are you okay?" I heard him speak, but couldn't see through my tears.

"She's... gone... best... friend... new... roommate... can't... handle..." I choked out.

Hani climbed into the fountain and cuddled up next to me. I dug my face into his chest. He put his arms around me.

"It'll be okay. Really. I promise. I'm still here. I'm not going anywhere. I'll always be here for you."

"What….about….." I couldn't get the words out.

"Shhhhhh… calm down now. Don't try to talk. Let's just sit for a while."

A few minutes later, Dean and Gretl appeared. I had stopped crying now, but was still sitting cuddled up in Hani's arms. Dean had his guitar with him. He sat down in the next arm of the fountain and began singing and playing.

We just sat listening to Dean 's music for what seemed like forever. The proctors let us have a free night due to the fact that only about 22 of us were around, so Gretl and I stayed up all night sitting in Dean and Hani's room, Dean playing the guitar.

The next day, I met my new roommates.

Chapter 15: Don't Mess With Texas

Annie was from Texas. Annie spoke on the phone to her boyfriend in Texas every morning before school, in the cloakroom during work time, after we got home, and late into the night. I hated Annie. My other new roommate, Tammy, didn't seem to pay attention to it. I, on the other hand, was not happy.

"She's always on the damned phone!" I yelled to Gretl. "I was supposed to call Kelsey two days ago, but that bitch is always talking to Texas."

"Calm down. It's only been three days since she moved in. Use my phone to call Kelsey," Gretl answered calmly.

After Kelsey left and Stella moved out, I practically lived in Gretl's room. Gretl's new roommates, Cameron and Tara, were really great. Cameron was from Rhode Island and Tara was from Washington State. We had bonded instantly. Gretl and I both missed the fall pages, but Cameron and Tara responded to that longing by asking us to tell our fall stories. Immediately reliving happy memories helped solidify our newfound friendships. After the first day, I felt as though Cameron and Tara had been around all year.

"I hate her. I really really hate her." I paced.

"I promise you guys that she's not always like this," Gretl apologized to her roommates.

"It's understandable. Every time I've gone into Natasha's room that girl's been on the phone. Who is she talking to anyway?" Cameron asked.

"Her boyfriend. In Texas."

"Why don't you tell her you need to use the phone at a specific time? Reserve it, see what happens?" Tara ventured.

"Maybe." I slumped down in a chair.

"Well, come on. We're supposed to go to that welcome dinner thing at Bullfeathers." Gretl pulled me out of my chair.

"What welcome thing?" I grumbled.

"It's a getting to know you reception thing, remember? We are supposed to meet the new pages," Gretl reminded me.

Aside from Gretl's and my roommates, I hadn't met most of the spring pages. They had been going through various orientations while the year pages had worked mostly as cloakroom and/or floor pages. I had been training as a cloakroom page, which meant I had spent hours trying to memorize all 200+ Democratic representatives. Each one had a photo flashcard with their name and state on the back. When I wasn't in the cloakroom or Gretl's room, I was with Dean and Hani. Well, mostly with Dean. Hani had been spending more time than usual with Michelle.

Bullfeathers was a pub/restaurant nearby. Most of the spring pages had gathered around the pool table. Annie wasn't there. She was on the phone.

"Howdy!" A red haired guy came over to us. "My name's Stan, I'm from Kentucky."

"Hi, I'm Gretl from Michigan. This is Cameron, Tara, and Natasha."

"What happened to the pigeon hand thing?" I asked Gretl.

111

"I'm over it," she said bluntly.

"Where are y'all from?" Stan asked.

"I'm from Rhode Island," Cameron said, "Tara's from Washington State and Natasha's from Los Angeles."

Stan looked at me funny. "Hollywood, eh. That's a scary place. You know, the Jews own Hollywood."

I blinked. "Really? I'm Jewish, but I promise I don't own any of Hollywood. My dad's a doctor."

He took a step back and turned pale.

"Are you alright?" I asked.

"I'm really sorry, but uh… I don't know if you're afraid of goin' to hell or nothin' but I can't take the risk." He turned and walked away.

"What just happened?" I asked Gretl.

"Got me," she said.

Stella came over and gave me a hug. "Hey there girl, how are the new roommates?"

"Don't get her started," Gretl rolled her eyes. "I'm going to mingle. See you in a bit."

"Stella, that guy from Kentucky just basically told me that he couldn't talk to me because I'm Jewish and going to hell."

"You're Jewish?" The thick southern drawl from a group of girls standing nearby forced my attention.

"Yes."

"Well, I don't wanna get personal or nuthin'. I'm Nancy, from Texas, by the way, but are you afraid of going to hell?" The girls giggled nervously.

I rolled my eyes, which were beginning to tear up, and turned away. What the hell was going on? All I did was come to a restaurant to meet people. Stella looked right at the girl and said, "Look, she's no different from the rest of us, so would y'ins just shut up?"

"Come on y'all. Let's go talk to some proper Christians," Nancy responded. I watched them cross the room to talk to Stan.

"Thank you," I said. I was so grateful to Stella. Prior to coming to DC, I had really never experienced any anti-Semitism. Stella hadn't met any Jews before me, but she never showed any negativity towards my religion. Five minutes of interaction with the new pages yielded more examples of prejudice than I had seen in my whole life. It did not bode well for the upcoming semester.

"Ignore them," Stella said. "They don't know what they're talking about."

"I think I hate Texans. My new roommate's from Texas. She's been on the phone since she got here."

"And the other one?"

"She hasn't said much to me yet, but she seems nice. She's an army brat and has lived all over the place. There she is, talking to Tara." Stella looked over at the six-foot tall African-American girl.

Hani came in and put his arm around me. "Hey, you guys. Aren't these people great! I like them all so much better than the fall pages!"

I stared at him. He liked them better that the fall pages? Was he crazy? Did they know he was Arabic? "I don't agree. Other than Gretl's roommates, I have not had…"

"Hani," Stan called. " Come over here ya A-rab!"

My jaw dropped as Hani left me and went over to Stan.

"Unbelievable." I shook my head. "I'm going home. I'm going to get that girl off the phone and call Kelsey."

"Wait, I'm going with you." Stella grabbed her coat.

I walked forcefully into my room, looked at my surgically-attached-to-the-phone roommate and declared, "You've been on the phone all day. I need to make a call."

She turned away, still talking.

"Did you hear me? I need to make a call."

"Pardon, I'm talking to someone," came the answer.

"Well, you can stop talking to someone. You've been talking to someone for hours, and I need to use the phone." At which point I slammed my hand down on the hang-up button and grabbed the receiver from her. I immediately dialed Kelsey's number. Annie and Stella both stared at me. Stella began giggling. Annie stomped out of the room.

"Holy shit!" I said into the phone, still caught up in amazement at my own actions.

"Hello?"

"Kelsey?"

"Yeah? Natasha? What's going on?"

"Natasha just went psycho on her new roommate," Stella called out. "Hi Kelsey!"

"Hey, there, tell her hi," came the voice on the other end of the line.

"She says hi. Wow, I can't believe I did that!"

"What did you do?"

"She had been on the phone for like three days straight so I got pissed off and hung up on her boyfriend."

Kelsey roared with laughter. "You didn't. Man, that's awesome!"

"I know! I don't believe myself. Well, you know what else happened? This new page, actually two of them, basically said they couldn't talk to me because I'm Jewish. The one guy said I was going to hell."

"He did what? Natasha, that's insane. And he told you to go to hell?"

"No, that I was going. You know, like the opposite of going to heaven."

"Are you serious? Wait a sec, that's not..."

"Kosher?" I tried to joke.

"Yeah. Seriously, if he's saying that and he just met you... where are these people from?"

"The guy who said I was going to go to hell is from Kentucky."

I could tell from the sound of Kelsey's voice that she was worried. If I hadn't been so caught up in my own self-pity, I might have recognized the ominous nature of these comments. Even at home in Michigan, Kelsey could see the way the wind was blowing far clearer than myself.

"Here, give me the phone, let me talk to her," Stella said.

Annie moved out the next day.

Chapter 16: Don't You Forget About Me

"Natasha? Some guy named Gus is here to see you. He's with someone named Ben." Cameron came walking into Gretl's room with the announcement. "They are at the front desk. They were going to call up to your room but luckily I was there and said you were probably in our room. Who are they?"

"Thank you! I'll go get them. Gus was dating a fall page, Katrina, and Ben is Kelsey's ex-boyfriend."

I raced downstairs and brought them up to the fourth floor lounge.

"So, have you heard from Kelsey lately?" Ben asked. Kelsey and Ben had broken up right before she left the page program and returned home to Michigan. Katrina and Gus were still technically dating.

"I've talked to Kelsey, but not Katrina. Has she called you?

"Yeah. It's been a few days, though. Hey, let's call them!" Gus said.

"There's only a pay phone out here."

"Well, can we call them from your room?" he asked.

"Guys aren't allowed in the girls' rooms. Or even in the corridor. Only in the lounge on the girls' floor." I replied.

"Oh, come on Natasha, your room is like two doors in. We'll run down there really fast. No one will notice."

"I guess we can. It has to be quick, though."

I have no idea what possessed me to agree, but before I knew it, Ben, Gus and I ran into my room. They called their girlfriends, we chatted for a bit, before it was time for them to go. I walked to the hallway door that opened towards the lounge. I held it opened. Ben came out and scurried into the common space. Gus began to leave, and realized that he forgot something. Just as he was about to exit my room, Maya appeared from the elevator.

"Hold it right there," she said.

"I can explain. They were just visiting and I was giving something to Gus, and…"

"Uh huh. That's it, party's over. You two leave. Natasha? Come with me."

She walked me down to the office and gave me restriction for the weekend. Three days, Friday, Saturday, and Sunday, I would not be able to leave my room after 7 p.m. I was surprised to find that I didn't really care. Ben and Gus had offered me a moment to go back in time. If it had been fall, I might have been furious at the prospect of not being able to leave my room for three days. However, it wasn't fall, and I felt like a part of me had been ripped away. I was only upset that I wouldn't be able to hang out in the park with Hani. Dean had gotten restriction that week for an alcoholic violation so he wasn't around at night anyway. I was just angry at myself for being stupid.

Why did I let them come down to my room? I wrote to Hani. Our math notes had resumed with an increasing regularity.

It won't be so bad. I'll come to the hall and wave at you from the door. He snickered. *It's only three days.*

Those other girls were on restriction for seven weeks! Dean has restriction for five!

I know, maybe I'll just call Kelsey and Jack and talk on the phone the whole time. I replied.

Will you call me? came the answer

If you're lucky.

You know, I think that new page Mindy wants me. He winked.

I don't know if I like most of these new pages.

You said that before. Give them a chance; they are really nice, he wrote, rolling his eyes at me.

I don't think they're nice. Do you know that guy Stan won't talk to me because I'm Jewish? And there's a group of girls from Texas that laugh at me whenever I walk in the room.

Give it time. Look, I'll come by tonight while you're on restriction. We'll talk. I'll be more careful than Gus.

My common sense told me that this was wrong. I knew he was dating Michelle. I had heard her bragging to the new pages about their wonderful relationship. He still rarely mentioned her to me, and still flirted with me endlessly.

And I still really liked him.

And he knew it.

Okay. I wrote. And the bell rang.

I sat in the doorway of my room staring out into the hall. I watched Michelle head out with the Texas girls. I saw Hani give her a hug and tell her to have fun. The hallway was deserted. My only roommate, Tammy, had gone out with Tara, Cameron, and Gretl to a movie.

118

They wouldn't be back for hours. It was Friday night with no WISP the next day. No one was around.

Hani beckoned from the door to the corridor. I raced over and unlocked it. He scurried into my room. We closed the door.

"So, I could really use a massage," he announced and flopped down on my bed.

"Is that a hint?" I asked, sitting next to him.

"Slightly."

I began rubbing his shoulders. The smell of his Drakar cologne hypnotized me.

"So do you like working in the cloakroom?" he asked.

"It's okay. I've memorized most of the congressmen at least." I gathered up every ounce of courage in my body. "What is going on with you, Hani? Are you dating Michelle?"

He turned his head towards me. I lay down next to him, looking into his eyes. They were amazing. Hazel. They almost looked blue against my pillow.

"I don't know. Who cares? I like you, though. You're a good friend."

"Just a friend?" I heard myself ask.

"I don't know," was his response. And he kissed me.

We stayed there for what seemed like an eternity. Suddenly, the hallway door slammed, jolting me back to reality. I pulled away. He sat up and leaned against the wall.

"Poor Michelle," he said. "She's a nice girl. I don't want to hurt her."

What about me? I screamed inside my head. Poor Michelle? Poor fucking Michelle? I tried to speak, but all I could do was look at him.

"I'd better go," he said, looking at his watch. "People are coming back. It's after 11 already. I don't want Michelle to see me here." He kissed me on the cheek.

"Make sure the coast is clear, would you?"

I poked my head out the door. No one was in the hall.

"It's clear," I said flatly.

"Come to my room next week. Sneak down. You know, they moved me out of Dean's room so I'd meet new people. I'm at the end of the hall now."

"Okay," I said. He left.

I called Kelsey.

"What am I doing?" I moaned into the phone.

"I have no idea. You'd better stop though. He actually said, 'poor Michelle'?"

"Yes. What do you think he meant? I mean, he asked to come down. He told me to come to his room next week."

"What did he mean? He didn't mean what you want him to mean, that's for sure. Look, you want to know my opinion? I think he's an ass. I think you're totally falling for a complete ass. I think you've been falling for the complete ass for months now, and what makes it worse is he knows you like him and he's totally taking advantage of it. It's getting late. Take a cold shower and go to bed."

"Thanks."

"No problem. Talk to you later," she said. I hung up the phone, hating her for being right.

Chapter 17: Lots of Bruhaha

"NATASHA! GET UP! GET OUT OF BED!" Tammy's army-like wake-up call jolted me out of a sound sleep.

"What's going on?" I yelped.

"Get your lazy butt out of bed already. It's after 6. You've been hitting that snooze button for 30 minutes now."

"I'm sorry, I'm just tired."

"Well maybe if you didn't stay up until 3 a.m. gabbing you would be more awake."

"Yeah..." I jumped in the shower and hurriedly got ready for school.

"Is she ready yet?" Tara poked her head inside our room as I was trying to tie my tie.

"Just about." I cringed.

"Come on, you can tie that later." Tara rushed me out the door.

"Tell that to Mrs. Caulfield. Last week she asked me if I was suicidal. It's all because I don't tie my stupid tie in the morning. There, I got it."

I made it to history class just in time for the bell.

"Close call," Hani whispered.

"Good morning, pages," Mr. Whitzal's voice boomed. "Today we will be discussing the ramifications of the Spanish-American War. Yes? Tammy?"

"Will we be talking about the actual war?"

"No. Any other questions? Good. Now, in 1900..."

I stopped listening. I was especially tired that day. I was feeling pretty low when Hani came into Math and sat next to me. I tried to manage a smile, but it came out all wrong.

I'm gonna run for page Vice-president. He wrote. Each semester we elected a president, vice-president, etc. of our page class. I had almost forgotten that a new class meant a new executive board.

Cool, I answered.

Vote Hani for V.P— It's as simple as that! Good for you, good for America, determined to work for you. Sounds like a TV ad, right? He seemed pretty impressed with himself.

I gave him a look.

Somehow I made it through school, got to work, and was told that I would not be in the cloakroom that day. I took some runs and headed out. I walked into Statuary Hall on my way to the Senate side, only to discover a large crowd of huge men and some sort of reception.

I saw Dean standing in the crowd and walked over to him. "What's going on?" I asked.

"The Dallas Cowboys are here. You know they won the Super Bowl, right? They are being honored."

"Oh." I didn't know. I should have, but I never really followed sports and had been too preoccupied with being in my own head to pay attention to much of anything.

"Excuse me, little lady." Congressman Pickle tapped me on the shoulder.

"Yes sir?" I asked loudly.

"What was that?" he replied. Oy. Hearing aid again.

"YES SIR?"

"Can you tell me which ones are the football players?" he asked. I stared at him for a moment wondering what to say. There was probably no one who knew less than I did about football players, but it did seem slightly obvious as to which individuals in the room were professional athletes.

"OKAY!" I yelled. I looked around at the huge men standing awkwardly in suits next to wimpy-looking congressmen and senators. I pulled Dean over. "Do you know who is who?" I asked.

"Yes? Why?"

"CONGRESSMAN PICKLE, THIS IS DEAN! HE CAN HELP YOU BETTER THAN I CAN!"

"Why, thank you kindly. I'm supposed to meet one of them… Emmett something. A color, um, blue was it? Maybe it started with an S?"

"Emmett Smith?" Dean was trying to stifle a laugh.

"That's the one. I don't follow this here sport so I just don't know which one he is."

I left Dean alone with the deaf congressman from Texas and headed to Senate Hart. On my way back, I passed through the old Supreme Court chamber. There stood Congressman Taylor, looking really lost.

"I'm so sorry, Natasha is it?" he asked, looking at my nametag. "Do you happen to know how I get to Senate Dirkson?"

I pointed him in the right direction and walked back towards the house floor. Giving directions had become a regular habit. Especially since the new class of congressmen had arrived. None of them, or their staff, knew their way around. When I got back to the House floor, I had a message to call home.

"Hello?"

"Natasha? Your brother's ankle had been getting worse, so we went to the doctor." My mother's voice sounded forceful. "He's been diagnosed with cancer."

"What?" I felt like my lungs had collapsed. "Are you sure?" My brother was eleven years old.

"We are waiting for some test results, and we are going to get a second opinion, but we'd like you to come home right away. He'll be having surgery next week. We will call you later to let you know your flight information."

I stumbled to my room in a daze and started sobbing hysterically. I remembered how my family had visited during the inauguration and how my brother had been limping around. I didn't know what to do with myself. I began pacing around my room. I called Hani, but he wasn't there. I called home about five times. My mother repeated what she'd told me about going for a second opinion and awaiting further test results. My brother would have surgery immediately to remove the tumor. I paced around my room some more–and called Hani again. He still wasn't there.

I walked into the common room, fighting back tears. Dean found me there. He brought me into the proctor's office, closed the door, and sat with me until I calmed down. He stayed with me for hours. When I had calmed down, we went out to the park where he played the guitar. It soothed me somewhat.

The next day I went home. My brother was standing smiling when I got off the plane.

"It's benign!" he yelled happily. The test results had come back that morning. He had the benign tumor removed and analyzed. It was only an aneurysmal bone cyst. I stayed home for a week, letting the sense of relief settle on my family. While I was in LA for that week, I turned 17.

Chapter 18: Under Police Investigation

"How could they do that? Who do you think did it?" Cameron was pacing angrily around the room.

"I bet it was that guy Stan. He's creepy," I answered, remembering our interaction that first day. It had been a month, and he still hadn't spoken to me. He acted as though I had rabies, moving as far away from me as humanly possible if for some reason we were forced to stay in the same room for longer than a minute.

"Stan's an ass, but do you think he'd really write that?" Cameron shook her head.

"What exactly did Billy say was written on his door?" Gretl demanded.

"KKK. It was written in pencil on the side of his door. He's black, he's gay, and he's from North Carolina."

"Oy vey," was all I could muster. Did he have one leg, too?

"I don't know," Gretl said. "That whole group of southerners are really conservative and just mean. Did you hear Nancy the other day?" She put on her best exaggerated southern drawl, "'Well my daddy'd shit six golden bricks if I brought a black man to the house.' It's disgusting."

That night I called Kelsey and told her about the KKK incident. She flipped out. "It really said that?" she gasped. "I am so glad I'm not still there. Wait till I come to visit. I'll give them a piece of my mind."

"I just hope they figure out who did it. I bet it's that guy Stan."

"That was the one who's anti-Semitic also?"

"Yep. He treats me like I'm a leper."

"Well, you know, religion is contagious, I've heard."

"Like mono?" I joked.

"Absolutely. Man, wouldn't want to catch the Jewish," she played along.

"Might go to hell by association." We both started laughing.

"You know, it's not funny. The situation you're in, it's really not," she said when we'd calmed down.

"I know. It's scary actually, and really sad. I feel sorry for them."

"Feel sorry for who?" Stella had walked into the room.

"Hey, I'm talking to Kelsey, I was telling her about what happened with Billy," I replied.

"Don't feel sorry for them. They don't deserve it. Whoever did that is nasty and that's all there is to it."

"What did she say?" came Kelsey's voice on the other end of the line.

"Here, I'll give you the phone," I said to Stella.

Stella was right. It was sad, but whoever was doing it was simply mean. The whole environment of the page program had changed. I noticed it even more clearly after I got back from seeing my brother in Los Angeles. I had a sense of fear that hadn't been there before, and with the exception of a small number of new pages, there existed an attitude that I didn't understand.

And then there was Hani. He never spoke to me when any of the new pages were around, but he had started calling me almost every day. He had sent me late Valentine's Day cards and birthday cards. He signed his

Valentine's Day card, "With Love, from your dear friend, Hani." The birthday card had been signed, "To Neigh-oo-mee, from your beloved friend, on your birthday. Love Hani."

In math, we had a few written conversations about Dean, which seemed to make him really angry.

Who does Dean like? I wrote once.

I don't know who Dean likes. Why do you keep talking about Dean? Do you like him or something? He glared at me when he passed it to me.

I was just wondering. I shrugged, *Anyway, can we study math Sunday? I'm lost.*

If you were paying attn you wouldn't be lost!!! Neigh-ooo-mee. Came his answer.

I am paying attn. I was annoyed now. *Can we meet? Or not?*

Probably, if I'm not getting laid. I have to find out if that girl Mindy likes me. I have a hunch she does, he wrote back. I felt my stomach tighten.

What about Michelle? I asked.

He rolled his eyes. The bell rang. "You're cute, but you have a lot to learn, Nat. Come on, sneak down to my room sometime. Seriously. We'll have a chance to... talk."

He kept asking me to sneak down to his room. But then he was never there when I called him. He was always off with Michelle. I didn't know what to make of it.

Within the last month and a half, my best friends had left, my brother had been diagnosed and then undiagnosed with cancer, and the new group of pages was, for the most part, one of the scariest, most conservative groups of people I had ever met. The labels "Conservative" and "Liberal" had suddenly taken on new dimensions. I found myself avoiding contact with anyone who called themselves "Conservative." On the same level, those people avoided "Liberals." It's funny to look back at our interaction. I've always been a Democrat, but I've never been terribly outspoken or politically active. I've always maintained that people have the right to their beliefs. I'm not gay, but I went to the gay rights march to support friends who were. I don't advocate having an abortion, but I'll be damned if anyone is going to tell me what to do with my body. I believe in gun control, but I eat meat, wear fur, and think fox hunting is cute (I like the red jackets). However, during my second semester of paging, if you spoke to some of the conservative pages, you would have thought my friends and I were more liberal than the entire student bodies of Berkeley and Columbia rolled into one. There weren't that many of us, and we were treated like freaks.

I found solace in Dean. He made me laugh, and he could calm me down. Although Dean had gotten in trouble for alcohol, we managed to spend lots of time sitting in the empty fountain, singing and playing guitar. Once he was finally off restriction, that time was able to last longer into the evening. Our guitar sessions had become my favorite part of the day. Dean didn't care what others thought about him. Unlike Hani. The more popular Hani became, the more distance there was between us. Math class became increasingly strained.

Sometimes Hani would make fun of Dean: *Why does everybody like Dean anyway?* He would scribble furiously. *His head is way too big, he looks like a girl, he's ignorant, childish, annoying and stupid. He has like 2 shirts, and 2 pairs of pants.*

I was slightly taken aback by his cruelty. *He's funny and has a great personality,* I responded.

Then he would talk to me about math class itself, or about Michelle, or about other girls he liked. He would always tell me to come to his room.

Dean told me to ignore him. He said that Hani didn't know what he wanted, and I was better off without him. Then Dean would sit with me and play "More than Words", and everything was okay again.

As okay as it could be anyway. The spring pages were polar opposites from the fall pages. Brittany, as clueless as she was, did not have a mean bone in her body. This group was flat-out racist. Gretl, Cameron, and I went to the Gay Rights March down on the Mall to show our support. All of us had gay friends.

As we left our building, Stan poked his head out from his window. Making sure he was loud enough for us to hear, he yelled, "Too many queers, not enough bullets."

The three of us stared at him, and then stared at each other. I was astounded that someone could say something so evil. It disgusted me that someone who would say that was someone I had to live with, and see every day. Finally, the prejudice issue reached its boiling point. A few days after the KKK writing was found on Billy's door, I got a call from Hani.

"Nat, guess what I'm doing!"

"What?"

"We're burning swastikas."

"You're what?" I repeated.

"We're making a statement about how much we hate the Nazis. It's a racial thing!"

"So you're burning swastikas? Where?"

"Here, in my room! It's great! Oh, gotta go Nat, Just wanted to tell you because you're Jewish and all and I thought you'd appreciate it! Later!"

I stared at the phone. "Did that just happen?" I said out loud.

"Did what just happen?" Tammy asked from her side of the room.

"I don't know. Never mind."

"No, what? I heard you say something about swastikas."

"Hani just called. He said he was burning them in his room. To make a statement against the Nazis. Those were his exact words."

She looked at me in shock. "Is he a complete idiot?" she asked.

"I'm beginning to wonder that myself."

"Let's tell the others," she said heading out the door.

We went into Cameron, Gretl, and Tara's room. Cameron was on the phone with a page named Sam, who was friends with Billy. She was trying to calm him down.

"It's alright, nothing is going to happen to you... I know, but they will take care of it.... Did you give it to a proctor? Good, then just wait, and calm down. Get some sleep. Okay? I'm sure this whole mess will work itself out. Goodnight, Sam."

"What happened?" I asked.

"Sam found a note stuffed under his door tonight." Cameron looked sad as she explained. "It said 'nigger lover.'"

Tammy gasped. My jaw dropped about five feet.

"He's friends with Billy. It must be the same person who wrote KKK."

"Natasha, tell them what Hani said!" Tammy demanded. Cameron and Gretl looked at me.

"Hani called. He's in his room burning swastikas," I responded heavily. "He said to make a statement against racism or the Nazis or something."

"What the hell is going on with this page class?" Gretl demanded.

"I don't know," I shook my head. "It's scary." There was silence for a minute as we allowed the events to sink in. Finally, I spoke.

"You know," I said sheepishly, "I really, truly thought... this is going to sound ignorant, but I really, really thought that racism was something that ended with Martin Luther King."

"Seriously?" Tammy ventured.

"Natasha, this is more than just racism," Cameron explained slowly. "This is full-on hatred. I mean, you're Jewish, so Stan won't talk to you. The KKK stuff obviously is because Billy is black and Chris is gay. And you know, Sam's gay too, and they're friends. This is hatred in its most extreme form."

"It's such bullshit!" Gretl stood up suddenly. I had never seen her so furious. "Burning swastikas? Shoving horrible notes under people's doors? We are all different, dammit! We are all from different places, and we are supposed to be in fucking Washington, the fucking capital of this country, because we are supposed to be the best. The. Best. It's damned hard to become a page. You have to go through all sorts of shit to get here. How the hell could they let such racist, bigoted, anti-Semitic assholes represent the country? It wasn't like this last semester, and Brittany had a fucking confederate flag! There's a difference between not knowing something is offensive, like she did, and purposely setting out to hurt people. And how could Hani take part in it? Natasha, he's supposed to be your friend and he's burning swastikas? Whatever lame ass excuse he comes up with, that's just fucked up!"

We all sat in silence, each of us finding a place within ourselves where we could figure out how to deal with the truth behind Gretl's anger.

The next day when we arrived at school, we were told to move into the English room for a meeting. Two men stood in front of the room with the teachers. Mr. Whitzal got up and began to speak.

"It has come to our attention, and the attention of the entire page staff, that there have been a collection of racial incidents. You all must understand that this is intolerance at its worst level. You are federal employees. You represent your peers, and that representation may not include bigotry. These actions will not be tolerated. You must accept each other as people. It is part of being a page, and more importantly, part of being a decent human being." He paused for a moment to survey our reactions. Stan was sleeping in the back of the room, and Nancy was passing notes to her friends. It made me sick.

"In order to best solve this situation, there will be an investigation," Mr. Whitzal continued. "These men," he announced, pointing to the strangers, "are federal officers. They will be interviewing some of you throughout the next few days. This situation will be resolved immediately; any prejudice, of any kind, will not be overlooked. You may go to class."

We sat down in history. Hani looked tired.

"I'll bet it's that Stan guy," I whispered to him. "You know he still doesn't speak to me, and it's just because I'm Jewish."

"Would you stop going on about Stan?" Hani snapped. "Dammit, what is your problem? Just because he won't talk to *you* doesn't make him evil. Stan's not a bad guy, and if you stopped thinking about yourself for five minutes you'd see that."

I sat, shocked and in silence for a full minute. How could he talk to me like that? Finally, I found my voice.

"Hani, what in the world were you doing burning..."

His attitude changed in an instant. "Shhh... don't say anything about that. I'm sorry I told you. We were just having fun. We didn't mean anything and we certainly didn't send any notes to anyone." He smiled at me. Somehow the smile didn't quite reach his eyes.

"Hey, I didn't mean anything by asking. It's just kinda strange, don't you think?"

He put his arm around me, and in his sweetest voice said, "I'm sorry for getting angry about Stan. You're not self-centered. But Nat? You won't tell anyone, will you? About my phone call last night?" He looked deeply into my eyes, pleadingly.

Kelsey would have told him to fuck off. Kelsey would have seen at that moment what kind of a person he was. Kelsey would have seen why he fit in so well with this group who went around flaunting their bigotry.

"No," I grunted. "I won't say anything."

"That'a girl." He smiled. His beautiful eyes seemed to twinkle.

Mr. Whitzal came into the room. "I think it's time to discuss the effects of prejudice in America." Hani didn't speak to or look at me for the rest of class.

Later that day, I was called to an office in Senate Dirkson. I sat at a table with three CIA agents. They asked me questions about the dorm. I answered as best I could. I told them about the comments I'd gotten about being Jewish. I didn't tell them about Hani's phone call.

Everyone was being interrogated, and a panic spread within the page class. Finally, at the end of the week, it was announced that one person was to be expelled from the program.

Dean.

"But why?" I asked him, sitting in the fountain.

"They think I did it," he answered. "I told them that I didn't think the KKK sign was written this semester at all. I think someone from Kentucky or Texas or something wrote it last semester on his own door as a joke. It's true. I'm sure I know who wrote it. It's not all that funny, but a few months ago it was meant to be a joke. We always used to say that this white guy, Jim, was so southern he must be a KKK member. It was funny because he wasn't remotely racist. I'm sure that's what it's from."

"And so they decided that you wrote it."

"They need a scapegoat. I'm an easy target. Look Nat, I'm not exactly a model page. I drink and had restriction for a few weeks. I used to sneak up to Whittany's room last semester before she left. I used to sneak her down here. I go out to the park to smoke when no one's looking. No one's caught me doing it, but they want to. I'm an easy scapegoat. Hell, I wasn't even here when they were burning swastikas and Sam got the note. I spent that night at a friend's house in Arlington. They have the records to prove it. But it's not good enough. I have to be out by tomorrow."

"Did Hani get in trouble for the burning thing?"

"He and three other guys got restriction for five weeks."

"It's still not fair, though, is it?"

"No, Nat. It's not."

He strummed his guitar softly. We sat in the fountain. It was cold out, but I couldn't feel it.

The news about Dean spread quickly. Many of the pages came out to the fountain to say goodbye. We had a massive song session as Dean played in our fountain for the last time. He climbed up to the top of the fountain with a cigarette hanging out of his mouth and screamed, "Goodbye Washington! Screw you all!"

The next day he was gone.

Chapter 19: Different Colored Socks

"Girls, you will be getting a new roommate," Julie announced to us, two days after Dean left.

"When?" I asked.

"Tomorrow," came the response.

"But Kelsey's coming to visit in two weeks," I protested. "Where is she going to sleep?"

"You have enough beds. It will be fine." It was true; we still had a bunk bed that nobody slept on.

We were curious about our new roommate. All we knew was that she was a Senate page.

The next day, while working in the Cloakroom, I answered a phone call from the president's office.

"Good afternoon, Democratic page service," came my standard reply.

"Yes, this is the office of President Clinton. The president would like to speak to congressman Traficant. Is he available?"

"One moment, please, I'll check." I left the Cloakroom and located the congressman on the side of the house floor.

"Congressman, the president is on the phone for you."

"Is he now? Well, you tell that liver-bellied son-of-a-bitch that I don't want to speak to him." Traficant turned around and walked in the opposite direction.

I was stunned, but obediently returned to the Cloakroom.

"Hello, sir?" I said slowly into the phone. "Congressman Traficant is... um... otherwise engaged. May I take a message?"

"Otherwise engaged, huh? Well, you tell that jack-ass freak-show of a rep that we're not going to take this much longer. Tell him to call the office ASAP." The line went dead.

I hung up the phone silently, staring at it for a moment. Gretl looked at me questioningly. I told her what happened. She laughed. "Yeah, they've been trying to talk to Traficant for ages. Just leave a message, and don't worry about it."

I was still reeling from the interaction when I returned to my room to greet my new roommate. Tammy met me in the lobby and we went up together.

"I'm Sue Ellen. It's nice to meet y'all," she said politely, as we came inside and threw down our bags.

"Hi there. I'm Natasha, and this is Tammy. I'm from Los Angeles; Tammy's an army brat."

"I'm saying Georgia right now, but you never know what will happen next week," Tammy joked.

Sue Ellen looked at us delicately. "I'm from South Carolina. I'm here because my uncle, Senator Strom Thurmond, said this'd be a good way to meet new people. Uh, such as yourselves." She smiled. She was very polite and very delicate.

"Your uncle is Strom Thurmond?" I asked.

"Yes. Do you know him?" she replied.

"I've seen him around."

Tammy and I exchanged looks as Sue Ellen became extremely busy unpacking. A bit too busy. She didn't seem overly eager to continue talking to us. I was in no mood to deal with someone who didn't want to talk to me, and Tammy was obviously not wowed by Sue Ellen. We left and went into Gretl's room.

"You guys will never guess who just moved into our room," Tammy exclaimed.

"Who? Oh, you guys got that new senate page. I heard she was from the south somewhere. Just what we need around here." Cameron rolled her eyes.

"That's not fair," Gretl frowned. "She just got here. Let's give her the benefit of the doubt. Come on, what's she like?" she asked.

"Well, let me put it this way. I don't think that Senator Thurmond's niece is happy about being in the same room as a Jew from LA and an African American army brat," I answered bluntly.

"She's a thurmondite?" Cameron gasped.

"I know." I rolled my eyes.

"Give her a chance, you guys," Gretl said diplomatically. "Natasha, you already kicked one southern roommate out of your room. You're gonna get a reputation for being prejudiced against southerners."

"Racist against racists. I suppose that's its own special kind of prejudice," I snickered.

"It is. Look, I'm as frustrated as anyone with all that's been going on around here, but the girl's been here 10 minutes. You can't possibly accuse her of being racist based on where she's from. That's just as bad as someone hating you because you're Jewish or from LA," Gretl pointed out.

She was right, of course. Intolerance has many faces.

"You're absolutely right," I agreed. "I promise to be nice. I will not hang up on any of her friends or family, nor will I judge her just because she is related to Strom Thurmond."

"Tammy? What about you? You have to live with her too," Gretl reminded her.

"I will not judge anyone unless I am judged," Tammy said firmly.

"Good." Gretl was satisfied. "Now, can we talk about something a bit more important? That new museum is opening up. The Holocaust Museum. Do you guys want to go?"

"Absolutely." I was really excited about the prospect of the National Holocaust Museum. Some of my extended family died in the Holocaust, and my entire family immigrated to the US from Eastern Europe. I remembered interviewing two older cousins for a school project. They were both Holocaust survivors; one had been a rebel, the other had been sent to Siberia. I was happy that the National Holocaust Museum was opening and couldn't wait to go.

"Good. Well it opens soon, and my congressman's office has offered to get me tickets, so I'll reserve them," Gretl said.

"You know, I only met my congressman once when my parents were here for the inauguration. I don't think his office is really too aware of me," I muttered.

"Really?" Cameron asked. "I see mine all the time."

"Well, I am the first page that my congressman has ever had. I don't think he really knows what to do with me. And he's busy. He's working on the Health Care bill with Hillary Clinton."

"Who is he?" Cameron asked.

"Waxman."

"Oh, yeah. The short guy."

"Yup. That's him. I've seen him around and I met him the once, but he's never spoken to me."

"That's crazy," Tara piped up. "I'm one of the Speaker's pages and he's taken me to lunch."

"Most people's members have. Mine hasn't. That's okay. I don't mind."

"You should call them and say hi," Gretl offered.

"I've done that. The reception has been slightly frosty." I sighed and looked at the ground. Then I changed the subject. "Hani asked me to sneak down to his room 'cause he's on restriction for 5 weeks. Should I?"

Kelsey's exact words had been: "ABSOLUTLEY NOT! IF YOU DO, YOU ARE A FOOL!" I tried to pretend that she just didn't understand because she wasn't here to see us together.

I had come clean about my crush on Hani. Or rather, it was so obvious to everyone that there was no point in trying to hide it. However, nearly every time I mentioned him, someone changed the subject. I wanted to hear that yes, of course I should go down there because he was absolutely in love with me and that the whole Michelle thing was just to throw everyone else off track. I wanted everyone else to see the wonderful notes that he passed me in math, and to hear the sweet things he said to me when we were alone.

But Hani always swore me to secrecy. I knew he'd be mad that I had even voiced the fact that I had a crush on him.

Silence filled the room as Cameron and Tara exchanged glances. After what seemed like an eternity, Tara spoke.

"I don't know," she replied hesitantly. "Wouldn't that be kinda funny? I mean, he's dating Michelle."

"I know. I don't really get him. But he told me to come down tonight," I said, trying not to act like the name Michelle made my stomach hurt.

"I don't think that's a good idea," Tara answered firmly. I was going to ask why but we were interrupted by Stella knocking at the door.

"Hey, what are y'ins up to? Do any of y'ins want to come with Janie and me to see this new movie that just came out? *Crying Game?*"

"Sure," was the overall response. I reluctantly left the Hani subject alone for the time being. After some debate, we decided to be nice and ask my new roommate if she wanted to come. We all went out of our way to be nice to her. She was polite, but quiet. And she hated the movie. The 'twist' in the movie caught all of us by surprise. We thought it was funny that the girl was actually a guy. Well, all of us except Sue Ellen. She didn't like DC, either. Although Tammy and I were perfectly nice to her, she called her uncle and went home within two weeks.

It had been a relatively calm winter, with hardly any snow. At least, I was told this was hardly any snow. I had lost at least six pairs of gloves and a few scarves. Then one day towards the end of March, the sky opened. I stared out the window. It was beautiful. I grabbed my jacket, my latest pair of gloves and raced outside.

It was night, and the snow looked like marshmallows against the pavement. I opened my mouth and felt the icicles melt onto my tongue. Everything was coated in white; the streets, the buildings, everything. I raced to the park across the street. The fountain looked like an ice sculpture. I stood there in the white silence for several minutes, letting myself get my first real taste of winter.

"You look like you've never seen snow before." Gretl and Cameron had seen me from their window and come outside.

"I have, but not like this. I mean, I went to Utah once to go skiing, but…"

"Once? You've only seen snow before once?" Cameron asked, amazed.

"No, I think I've seen it two or three times. I've gone to Vermont at wintertime before. I've never actually lived in snow though. Isn't it beautiful?" I replied.

"It is until you have to shovel a driveway," Gretl commented.

"Have you ever made a snow angel?" Cameron looked at me questioningly.

"What's that?" I asked. I watched as she lay down in the snow and moved her arms and legs up and down. Then she stood up and looked at where her body had been.

"That's amazing!" I sucked in my breath at the image of an angel in the snow. "I want to try!"

We stayed outside for a while making snow angels and snowmen. A few days later, it stopped snowing, and the weather began getting warmer. Every day we would go out into the park and play in the snow. Even as it warmed up, there were still piles that had crystallized in the overnight cold that accompanied the daily bouts of sunshine. I thought back to my first taste of autumn. Feeling the snow, the cold... I marveled at the many faces of nature I missed living in LA. Each season forced the stone buildings to take on a different personality. The white stone buildings blended into the background as the snow fell. As the snow melted, it was as if the buildings themselves came out of a cocoon, allowing themselves to be seen again.

Chapter 20: Aw, Norman

"You're here!" I yelled as I tackled Kelsey before she fully emerged from the cab.

"I told you I'd come visit," she said, hugging me tightly. "And I brought pictures from home, of my family and my dog, Norman. You'll love them."

We headed upstairs.

"What happened to your new roommate?" she asked when we got to our room.

"I guess I scared her off," was my response. "I have that way with people."

"Seriously, Natasha, what is going on? Stella, you, and I lived just fine together, and now you've lost two roommates in three months? Some people would call that careless."

"Tammy and I get along well," I defended.

"Yeah, that's good. But what happened with Sue Ellen?"

"I really don't know. I mean, we are all sort of walking on eggshells after the racism incidents."

Kelsey nodded. "I'd like to meet that guy Stan. I have a few things I'd like to talk to him about."

"I'll see what I can do, but he generally stays away from me. Which is just fine."

"I know. I just want to have some fun. Do you think he's out in the park? I saw a few people head out there when the taxi was driving up."

"Maybe," I shrugged. "Let's get Stella and go see."

Stella was more than happy to let Kelsey meet Stan. She wanted to make sure we introduced Kelsey to

Nancy, too. We all went out to the park where people had gathered in various patches and corners to hang out for the afternoon. Sure enough, Stan and Nancy were with Michelle and Hani and a few other Republican pages in one corner of the park. Stella and I hid behind a bush nearby while Kelsey marched up to them, presumably to say hello.

"So, Kelsey, you're here? To visit?" Hani said, surprised. I hadn't told him about her visit. He never really gave me the chance. Even in math our notes had been about Dean, or the police investigation, or whatever was bothering him.

"Yep. Hi there, how are you? Hi, Michelle."

"Hi. It's a surprise to see you," Michelle offered politely.

"How do you like that?" Kelsey turned to Stan, who was standing next to Michelle. "I'm gone for three months... no, not even, two months, and they've forgotten all about me. You would never do that, would you?" she said sweetly.

"Lordy, no way. I'm Stan. It is a pleasure to meet you." He stood, beaming. We could hardly keep ourselves from laughing. Stan had a reputation for being a flirt, and Kelsey with her red hair and green eyes, was gorgeous. She snuggled up to Stan.

"Well, that is the sweetest thing I could ever hear."

"I'm a sweet guy."

"I'll bet you are," she flirted.

"You know what, I think you are desperately in need of some good ole southern hospitality." Stan moved in closer.

"I'm sure I do. It's been so long since I had anything that I might call... hospitable. And every girl needs hospitality. Don't they, honey?" She batted her eyes at Stan, and then looked over at Nancy.

"I'm sure I don't know what you mean," Nancy answered coldly.

"Oh, posh. I'm sure you do." She moved in closer to Stan. "We know what hospitality means, don't we, sweet cheeks?"

"Lordy, ma'am, we absolutely do. Now, I'm thinking that you need..."

"You know," she interrupted, looking at him intently, "you remind me of my best friend."

"I remind you of a girl?" he asked, confused.

"No, silly. My best friend's a guy. He's gay, of course. He is just a riot, and always says things like, 'lordy' this and 'lordy' that. He's Buddhist, and his family's half-Chinese, half-black. He has like six brothers and sisters, and he's the youngest, so he has a few nieces and nephews. Especially from his one brother, who converted to Orthodox Judaism when he got married. His family's great; one of his sisters is Catholic now. She's a nun, has been ever since the accident. But I just love him! Seth. Hey, Stan, your names even start with the same letter! What a coincidence." She laughed and threw her arm around Stan's waist, who stared at her hand like he had just noticed a large spider crawling up his side. But Kelsey wasn't done yet.

"You know, Seth and I are looking to go to college together. We've been thinking about going to the University of Vermont because we heard a rumor that they're going to legalize gay marriage up there, and he really is so in love with his Muslim boyfriend Hassan. I heard Vermont's a great place to meet men. I mean, I was dating this guy here, Ben. Oh, you know him, Michelle, Hani, don't you? Isn't he sweet? You know, I usually date black guys, but Ben was so wonderful, I made an exception. Do you know his father's family is Cuban? They snuck here through Florida." She looked at Nancy. "You're Hispanic, aren't you?" Kelsey asked, squinting at her. Nancy shook her head violently, her lips tightly pursed. "Oh, my bad. You look Hispanic." Nancy eyes nearly bulged out of her head. It looked like she might be sick.

Kelsey turned back to Stan, a wide smile on her face. "See, Ben's father ended up in Miami, and that's where he met Ben's mother, who was actually a stripper at the time. Isn't that romantic? I heard it was love at first sight! Oh, I can't wait to see him later. I really want to introduce him to Seth one day, too. I just think they'd get along famously. Oh well. Must go. I have to find Natasha. We're going to have a Passover Seder together later! I just love Jewish holidays. Ta ta!"

Kelsey left Stan with his jaw on the ground. Nancy looked like she'd been hit over the head with a mack truck. Hani and Michelle (whom Kelsey never found worth talking to when she was a page, so therefore had no reason to think that one ounce of her story was untrue) also seemed to be in a state of shock. Stella and I snuck away from the stunned group to the other side of the park to meet Kelsey. She had a huge smile on her face. We managed to contain our hysterics until we got up to my room, where our laughing fit lasted almost an hour as we rehashed every detail of Kelsey's new "best friend."

At one point, Gretl and Cameron came in and asked us what was so funny. We tried our best to relate Kelsey's story, complete with the others' reactions.

"Are you serious? Can I bow down to you? That is so brilliant!" Gretl shrieked.

"Stan looked like he'd just met the devil! You should have seen the look on his face by the time she was done!" I managed, tears of laughter streaming down my face.

"Is it too late for me to do something like that?" Cameron asked eagerly. "Maybe I can be a bisexual transvestite from France!" We roared with laughter.

When we finally calmed down, Kelsey looked around the room. "You know," she said, "it's funny, but it's not funny. The fact that those people are so damned close-minded really isn't funny. I feel bad for you guys that you have to deal with them for the semester. I mean, I'm only here for a week and I'll play it up as much as possible, but you guys have a few more months."

"I know," Gretl replied sadly. "And you know what's worse than that? The fact that we are all from the same country. I mean, I was so proud last semester. Of all of us, of our country. I mean, we embraced our differences. How can people in a place that is supposed to be free, and allow for so many different types of freedom, have so much hatred for things that they don't know?"

"It's because they don't understand," I answered. "Haven't you guys read *1984*? People fear what they don't understand. I never thought that was true, but I also thought that racism ended with Martin Luther King. In LA, everyone is a mish-mosh of different things. I almost feel sorry for them. I mean, they have to go through life being afraid. And they are expressing that fear through hatred that doesn't even have any truth. And what pisses me off about this is that someone like Hani, who I used to think was really open-minded, can't seem to see how dangerous that is."

Kelsey whipped around to look at me. "Hani *is* dangerous," she declared flatly. "He is totally fucking with your mind. And he has been all year."

"I don't know if I'd go that far," I said, feeling hurt.

"I would." Kelsey looked around. "What do you guys think?"

Before anyone could answer, the phone rang. It was Jack. He had come to visit and was staying with some of the other year pages. We raced into the common room to see him. I gave him a huge hug.

"Hey! When did you get here?" I asked.

"About a half hour ago. You know, I was supposed to stay with Hani, but his new roommate, some guy named Stan, took one look at me and said I looked too much like a hippie for him to be able to deal with having me in his room, so I'm staying with some other guys. Is he the asshole you told me about?" Jack asked.

"Yes! You have to hear what Kelsey did!" I laughed, and we filled him in on the events of the day.

The week that Kelsey and Jack were there was an enormous stress reliever for all of us. Most of the spring pages stayed away from us, which was just fine. Hani stayed away too, which kind of hurt. Jack pointed out that Hani had gained a certain popularity that he hadn't had in the fall. It made Jack uncomfortable to spend too much time on the guy's floor. As a result, we stayed away from Annex 1 as much as possible.

Kelsey and Jack met us at work nearly every day. The Capitol Hill police officers remembered them and let them come visit us on the floor. One day, Kelsey and I were walking towards Rayburn when we bumped into the gorgeous Congressman Taylor.

"Good afternoon, Congressman," I said.

"Hello there, Natasha. And Kelsey, correct? You worked in Ways and Means."

"That's right," Kelsey answered, impressed. "It's nice to see you again."

"I know this year is short for you girls, but I meant to tell y'all. If you need college recommendations, feel free to contact my office," he said.

"Thank you," I replied astonished. "That'd be great."

"Absolutely, thank you!" Kelsey exclaimed.

"Don't mention it. You girls are a real help around here. It's my job to let you know that's appreciated."

We stared as he walked down the hall. Somehow we managed to contain ourselves until we got outside the building, at which point we jumped up and down, screaming for a few minutes with excitement.

The National Holocaust Museum finally opened, and Gretl got us all tickets through her member's office. The group of us gathered in the lobby, getting ready to go.

"Where are you all off to?" Hani came in with Michelle.

"The Holocaust Museum," Kelsey responded.

"Really. Hmm... interesting," Hani responded, barely suppressing a grin.

"What was that about the Holo... oh, it's you." Stan had come into the lobby. He took one look at Kelsey and backed away.

"Hey, boy, you need to go through the metal detector if you want to come inside." Officer Rude glared at Stan from behind the police desk.

"I was about to. And don't call me boy, you..." His voice faded as the African American Capitol Hill police officer stood up. At 6'5", Officer Rude towered over Stan.

"What was that?" he demanded.

"Nothing," Stan mumbled.

"Coward," Kelsey said frankly. She turned to me. "See, the southern boy acts all tough, but since he knows he's full of shit, he freaks out at the slightest hint of anyone standing up to him." She tuned back towards Stan. "Bye, you weak, slimy, close-minded asshole."

Stan stood dumbfounded. As we got outside, we heard him yell, "Bitch!"

Kelsey stopped walking, turned around, and marched back inside. "Say that to my face." She waited for a moment. Stan stared in silence. "You can't, can you? See, I can say this, because I'm leaving tomorrow and I don't give a shit what you think about me, but you are by far the biggest jerk-off I've ever met."

"Hey. You don't know anything. Leave him alone," Hani yelled at Kelsey.

Kelsey turned to face Hani. "What? You need to defend your poor stupid friend because he's too chickenshit to say things to my face? What about how *he* treats other people? What about how he treats people that you pretend to be friends with? Some friend you are. Well, I'm going to the Holocaust Museum now to share with *my* friend the experience that her family went through because of prejudiced assholes like Stan here. But you're not going to go. No. You sure know how to choose sides. Go upstairs now, fuck your ugly girlfriend, and burn some more swastikas while you're at it. Later." She marched back out and didn't stop moving until we got to the metro station.

"Wow, that was awesome! I'm so impressed!" Jack gave Kelsey a hug.

"What is up with Hani these days?" Gretl shook her head.

"I wish I knew," I mumbled. "That was great, Kelsey. Thank you."

"Don't mention it. Good luck dealing with him after tomorrow, though."

"Stan?" I asked.

"No, I think Stan will keep his distance. He's too much of a baby to ask for confrontation, and too afraid of what you might do to retaliate. It's Hani that I'd worry about. Something tells me he's up to something, and I'm afraid for you."

"He's never done anything bad to me," I argued.

"That you know about. Keep your eyes open. That bastard's sleazy. Watch yourself."

We got on the train and went to the museum. Once inside, we saw piles. Piles of shoes, piles of suitcases... piles of things that once belonged to people. People like me. Maybe even my relatives. Things that were taken away as they walked to their death in the gas chambers. Rooms of death, created by people who lived in fear. Fear of anything different. There was a wall which had the different patches people were given by the Nazis. Yellow Stars of David for Jews, pink triangles for homosexuals. Badges for Catholics, badges for gypsies, for socialists, for the mentally or physically ill. Labels that designated the reason each wearer was denied the right to live.

When we got to the room that held a set of bunkers from Auschwitz, there was an elderly woman staring from the side into the bunks.

"They seemed much smaller at the time," she said quietly. We turned to look at her. She looked around at the faces that questioned without asking. Begging her to tell her story. She smiled gently. "They seemed so much smaller when so many of us were made to share them." She took her daughter's hand, and they walked away.

I stood in silence looking at the bunkers, imagining the frail woman lying inside one. I felt tears rolling down my face. Jack came over and put his arm around me, leading me to the next room. I felt so grateful for everything I had, and so happy that my friends could share this with me. We didn't speak for a long time after leaving the museum, each of us contemplating the emotions the museum had evoked in us.

The next day, Kelsey and Jack left to go home.

Chapter 21: Conference Calling

I didn't see any signs of retaliation in the days after the incident between Hani and Kelsey. Hani just kept begging me to come to his room. So, I began sneaking to his room despite myself. Somehow, after Dean was kicked out and Jack and Kelsey's visit ended, I found myself really lonely again. Hani knew it, and he knew how much I liked him. Sometimes we just talked. Sometimes we did math or history homework. Sometimes we sat in silence, just cuddling.

"You will do a notebook detailing the Industrial Revolution in America in the 1920's." Mr. Whitzal's announcement meant little to me. I had really not tried hard in school and still managed to maintain an A average. School was easy. This project was really no different than anything else.

That night, Ben, Kelsey's ex-boyfriend, came to visit. Tara, Cameron, Gretl, and I sat talking to him in the park. It was a Friday.

"I love Pink Floyd's *The Wall*." Cameron's eyes brightened.

"It's so awesome. The way everything is presented is amazing," Ben agreed. He and Cameron had gotten along famously. They ignored the rest of us, talking for a few hours.

"It's after 11," I pointed out. "We have to go in soon. Curfew."

"That so totally sucks!" Cameron moaned. "Hey, I have an idea. What if we snuck you in? You'd have to stay the night, but if we just hid you until after the proctors came around, then we could talk all night!"

"Not in our room," Gretl said frankly. "I don't want to take the chance."

'What about in your room, Natasha? It's such a mess, I'm sure we could find a place to hide Ben without anyone noticing." Cameron looked at me eagerly. I didn't want to say no. She had been a good friend, and I didn't mind having Ben around.

"Sure, why not."

We headed to the front door of our building. Gretl walked right in, ignoring us. She wanted no part of the rule breaking. Tara and Cameron kept Officer Rude busy while I snuck Ben inside and up the stairs. We made it to my room without anyone noticing. Well, almost anyone.

"Is that a boy in your room?" Michelle's head peeked into my room just as we got inside.

"What's it to you?" Cameron looked at her.

"Nothing." She shrugged and left.

"I'm Tammy, by the way." My roommate had been reading on her bed.

"Hi, I'm Ben."

We hid Ben in the closet while the proctors did a room check. Cameron and Ben snuggled on the extra bed. Tara, Tammy, and I decided to leave them alone. We decided to go to Stella's room since it was in the same wing as mine. Their room was on the other side of the floor.

"There you are!" Janie raced in a few minutes later, flustered.

"What's going on?" I asked.

"I just heard a rumor. Is Ben in your room?"

"Yeah, so? He's with Cameron."

She shook her head as if she needed to catch her breath. "Michelle called the proctors and told them you had a guy in your room. You better get down there!"

"What?" I yelled, rushing out the door. As I got into the hallway I saw Julie walking into my room. Cameron was calmly standing at the door.

"I'm here because I was borrowing some clothes. Natasha told me to just come in and take whatever I wanted," she was saying.

"And no one is in the room with you?"

"No, why?" Cameron asked innocently.

Julie gave her a stern look.

"What's the matter?" I asked, trying to control my voice.

"We've gotten a report. I must search your room." She began looking all over my room. She looked in the bathroom, then in the study room. She looked into the closet, picking up all the clothes that were on the floor—the clothes we had hid Ben under for room inspection. But he wasn't there. Then she looked under my bed. In looking under my bed from the front, all she saw were my suitcases. I had three big ones, which seemed as though they took up all available floor space under the bed. She examined the space closely, but there was no Ben. Where did she put him? I thought. Did she throw him out the window? I'm on the fourth floor. The image of Ben hanging from a drainpipe fluttered through my mind. Julie stood in the center of the room, thinking.

"I suppose it was a false alarm," she finally said. As she headed towards our door, she stopped and looked one more time at my bed. Her gaze alternated between the wall and the bed.

"What is behind those suitcases?" Julie looked one more time at the huge suitcases.

"The wall," I shrugged.

"Hmm. Do you mind?" She pulled the bed out from the wall. Lying there, on his side to make him as thin as possible, was Ben.

"Natasha, you'll have to come with me." Julie smiled triumphantly. "And you, my friend, are trespassing on federal property. I'm afraid I'll have to have you arrested."

"Are you serious?" His eyes were wide.

"Perfectly."

Sure enough, as I shuffled down to the proctor's office, Ben was carted away by Capitol Hill police officers. I was awarded restriction for two weeks. Ben spent the night in jail.

"What happened?" I asked Cameron the next day. We were sitting in the park. I hadn't had time to ask, but Ben had called me in the Cloakroom to tell me what happened afterwards. When they refused to let him talk to me, he called Cameron. Later, I called him back on my room phone. He was mad. And understandably. I would have been pissed off too if I had gotten arrested for trespassing in a federal office building.

"We heard that Michelle had called the proctors, so I hid him," she said sheepishly. "I'm sorry I asked you to let him go to your room."

"It's okay. He's furious, though. I can't believe he spent the night in jail!"

"Who spent the night in jail?" Hani came up behind me.

"Ben. Kelsey's ex." I raised an eyebrow.

"Oh, yeah. Michelle told me that something happened."

"Michelle called the proctors on him. He's really pissed, and he has every right to be. He was arrested for trespassing, for Christ's sake." I glared at Hani. It wasn't his fault, but the fact that his girlfriend was responsible was infuriating.

"Is he mad?" Hani asked.

"Of course he's mad," Cameron snapped. "Wouldn't you be? This goes on his permanent juvenile record. He'll have to have a hearing. I'd be mad too."

"Do you think he'd do anything to Michelle to get back at her?" Hani asked, furrowing his brow.

"I don't know. He has a right to be angry." I shrugged. "I'm pissed off, too. I have restriction for two weeks. But compared to Ben, I got off lucky."

"Oh, poor you," Hani snapped sarcastically. "I have restriction for five."

"I know. I'm sorry. It just really sucks."

"Tell me about it." He walked away.

"Why is he so self-centered?" Cameron demanded. "He brought his restriction on himself. It's Michelle's fault that you got in trouble and Ben got arrested."

"I don't know. I don't get him." I shook my head. Cameron sighed.

Later that day, Julie came to my room.

"Natasha, I must tell you that although we weren't planning on it, we are now going to have to call your parents and your congressman regarding your actions."

I was dumbfounded. "My congressman? Why? I'm serving my restriction."

"It's not that. It's... well, I personally find this hard to believe, as we have had no real problems with you this year, but there has been a report that the boy has communicated threats through you to one of the other pages."

"Huh?"

"Has the boy expressed any vindictive sentiments regarding any other pages?"

"He's mad about spending the night in jail, but he hasn't threatened anyone," I responded, completely baffled.

"Natasha, can I be honest with you?"

"Yeah?"

"I would be careful about what you say around here. Somehow one of the other pages seems to have gotten the distinct impression that she has been threatened. Can you think of why?"

I thought about my conversation with Hani. *Do you think he'd do anything to Michelle to get back at her?* I remembered his question. And I said I didn't know.

"No," I responded.

"Well, just don't let me catch you with any other guys in your room." Julie smiled.

I spent my restriction listening to Bob Dylan, eating take-out Chinese food, and working really hard on the history project. It was due right after my restriction ended. I had finished it in advance so I could celebrate my freedom.

"Hey, have you done that project yet?" Hani asked the Friday before it was due.

"Yeah. I'm going out tonight. And this whole weekend for that matter. Of course I finished it."

"I'm not really sure what I'm doing. Can I look at yours?" he asked. "I'll give it back to you tomorrow. I promise."

"Yeah. Just as long as I get it back." I went to my room and got it for him. He gave it back to me on Sunday and that Monday, I handed it in.

Tuesday, Mr. Whitzal handed it back to me with a great big 0 written on it. I was mortified.

"Um, Mr. Whitzal? Why is this a 0? I thought I did the assignment. I actually worked really hard on it."

"Cheating is not permitted in this class," he answered.

"What? I didn't cheat. I've never cheated!" I exclaimed in a state of shock.

"'Then do you mind explaining to me why you and your friend over there handed me the exact same work?" I spun around to see Hani standing sheepishly at the door.

"We worked on it together," he answered. I was still speechless.

"This was not a group project," Mr. Whitzal answered.

"I know, I didn't realize we both wrote down so much of the same thing," Hani explained.

"Is that right, Natasha?" Mr. Whitzal looked at me.

I stared at Hani, who had a pleading look on his face. "We worked on it together," I repeated tonelessly.

Mr. Whitzal sighed, "I admit, Natasha, that I was surprised. You normally do excellent work, participate in class, and are knowledgeable about the subject matter." He thought for a moment. "This was not a group project, and I must penalize you, but since this was a first offense, I will give both of you a C instead of a 0."

"Thank you, Mr. Whitzal," I managed.

"Yeah. Really, thank you. It won't happen again," Hani blabbered.

"It better not." He looked at me, raising an eyebrow. Hani left the room quickly. I gathered my books, heartbroken.

"Natasha," Mr. Whitzal whispered, "I know this is your work. Do yourself a favor, and keep your material to yourself from now on. I'm sorry to have to penalize you, but I'm sure it will help you think twice about letting anyone else see anything you've done."

Tears welled up in my eyes. "Thank you. I will. I know I will," I muttered.

In math class, Hani handed me a note.

Natasha,

I know that you probably hate my guts right about now, but please don't be mad at me; and I can understand why, but please don't be mad at me. The last thing I need right now is a good friend of mine to be mad at me. Think of it this way. At least you're in my shoes; Nelson is totally screwing my grade and so is Bowen. Natasha, I'm so sorry. I can totally understand if you never want to talk to me again. Please don't mention this to anyone; it's kind of personal.

Love,

Hani
P.S. Please don't hate me.
P.P.S. If there is anything I can do, don't hesitate to ask.

I stared at the letter through most of class. It wasn't until a few hours later that I was able to respond.

"How could you do that to me?" I demanded.

"Please, Nat... You will forgive me, won't you?" he started.

I sighed. I didn't want to forgive him, but I knew I wouldn't be able to stay angry with him either.

"I'll have to think about it." I walked out of the cloakroom and over to the Speaker's office. Tara was sitting at the front desk. I explained to her what happened.

"What does the note say?" she asked.

I showed it to her.

"I guess he's sorry. I mean, I'm not telling you to forgive him, but maybe he means well in writing this."

"Yeah, I guess. I just... I don't know. Why is this 'personal?' Why doesn't he want me to tell anyone?" I wondered aloud.

"He's weird. I don't know," she shrugged.

It took me the rest of the week, but I forgave him right before we left for spring break.

Chapter 22: Allergic To Spring

Spring break went too fast. I did not want to go back to DC. It was mid-April.

"I only have to make it to the beginning of June," I said to myself. As soon as I got to my room, I took a bright orange marker and began a backwards countdown.

"Looking forward to leaving, I take it," Tammy laughed from across the room.

"Just a bit." Walking down the hall was painful. Recently I had caught a couple of sideways glances from people, which made me feel a bit awkward. I looked forward to going on my runs just to get away from the page desk. I didn't understand why people were looking at me so strangely.

"What is going on?" I asked Hani in history class.

"What do you mean?" He didn't look at me as he asked.

"Why are people looking at me like that?"

"It's all in your mind," he retorted. Then in math, he wrote, *You forgave me, right? You're not still mad at me? I care about you so much, I couldn't take it if you were.*

You know I'm not, I wrote back. *Listen, can I be honest with you?* I got really nervous.

Hmmm? He wrote.

I wrote this for you. I handed it to him.

I had written him a letter detailing all the things I was feeling. I had waited to give it to him because he was so standoffish half the time, and the other half he acted like he was my best friend. The signals he was giving me were so mixed, I needed clarification. My letter was as honest as possible. I told him how much I cared about him, and that I didn't understand why he acted the way he did. I had done everything that he ever asked of me. It hurt that he pushed me away when other people were around, but then when he needed me, he would race to my side. I thought that his letter about the history notebook was proof that he really did care, but now I wasn't so sure. I was sad and depressed and I needed him now more than ever. I needed him to be there for me the way I was for him.

I watched him read it. He put it down with no expression on his face and turned back to the lesson. A few minutes later I wrote, *Do you have an answer or an opinion on anything I just told you?*

He thought for a moment before writing, *Not really.*

I felt the wind go out of my stomach. *Do you care?* I wrote.

YES, came the response.

I'm scared. I trembled as I wrote the words. My loneliness had gotten the best of me.

That's dumb, was his answer.

I got really annoyed. *I'm not dumb. Just scared.*

You shouldn't be, was his answer. Then the bell rang. I sat alone in the room for a moment, taking it all in. What just happened? Frustrated, I rushed to my locker and ran over to work. I was determined to do as many runs as possible so as to get lots of points in a hurry. I wanted to go home, and the only way to do so was to have the largest number of points. I grabbed run after run. I took whips—packages with the bills for the week—and "Floor Todays," a bulletin saying what would be discussed that day. Then I took a bunch of flag runs and some runs to the Senate side. I bumped into Congressman Taylor, whose friendly, dazzling smile calmed me a bit. By one in the afternoon I had so many more points than everyone else that Mrs. Donnelly let me go home.

I threw my bags in my room and went to the park. They had turned the water on in the fountain, so I couldn't sit in it anymore. That was fine anyway; it was no fun without Dean. The park had taken on a new life. Pink and yellow tulips had grown, seemingly out of nowhere. They lined the paths and covered the sides. The newly re-grown grass offered a brilliant contrast to the flowers. The pastel landscape was capped by the light that bounced off the water that sprang from the fountain. The whole park seemed alive with newfound energy. My sorrow had no place in the beauty that had sprouted where winter had been not so many weeks before.

I ran over to the side wall where I knew I'd be hidden by the newly blooming bushes. I slumped to the ground. I'm stronger than this! I screamed inside my head. What is going on! I put my head in my hands. A few minutes later, Stella appeared from around the side.

"I saw you come here. What's wrong?" she asked calmly. I shook my head, at first unable to answer.

"I don't cry. I never used to cry. I don't know what's going on. All I seem to do is cry and I'm sick of it," I sniffed angrily.

"I can tell you why you're crying, and I also can tell you that it's okay," she stated frankly. "All this stuff.

Living here, everything. It's hard. And honestly, I don't know what's going on with you and Hani, but it seems like that's just making it worse."

"I don't know either. One second he's begging me to be with him every moment of the day; other times he acts like he can't stand me. I just can't figure out what's going on! Stella, I'm such a failure. I can't do anything right."

"That is not true." She stood up. "Alright, well, maybe you were when you got here, but you are the furthest thing from one now. Look at all the things you've done."

"Like what?" I choked.

"Laundry, dishes, learning football players' names," Stella smiled. "Hell, you are one of the most open-minded people here this term. That's what's killing you. These people, they just don't know much about anything, and they're not willing to learn. The fall pages, we wanted to learn. That's why you and I stayed. To learn more. People like Hani are just taking advantage of a group of close-minded conformist bigots. He loves it. Why? Because people worship him instead of ignoring him or making fun of him like they did last term. You know how he was kind of a loner last term? People teased him. I know you didn't see it that much, but a bunch of the pages were always teasing him. Now there are so few people here who understand that he does not have one original thought in his body. You know that birthday card you showed me? Where he wrote your name all funny? He only did that because Dean wrote it that way first."

"That's true." I laughed a bit, wiping the tears from my eyes.

"Listen to me." Stella took a deep breath and looked at me intently. "Hani talks about you behind your back. He's been going around telling people that you follow him around. That you worship him and he can't get you off his back. That's why he's so strange with you—one minute being your best friend, the next minute pushing you away. Having you appear to worship him makes him seem cooler. He's playing you and Michelle against each other."

I felt like I had been punched. Would he really do that? "How do you know?" I asked, my heart pounding.

"Janie's on the Republican side. I always forget because she's so not a Republican. That's why she hangs out with us. But regardless, that's where she reports to work. She heard Michelle talking."

"Did Janie talk to Michelle?" I asked.

"No, that sneaky bitch wouldn't give Janie the time of day. No, Michelle was talking to some of her fellow conservatives. She was telling them..." Stella hesitated, looking like she was deciding how much to tell me. "She said that you were pathetic for following her boyfriend around, and that you needed to get a life. She said that Hani told her how he couldn't understand why you didn't listen to him, and that he kept asking you to leave him alone."

"That bastard." I felt like I was going to be sick. "How can he say that? He's such a liar!"

"He's messing with your mind, and using you as a pillowcase," Stella replied.

I was angry. I thought back to his letter about the notebook. *Don't mention this to anyone, It's kind of personal,* he had written. Then I thought about Julie asking me if Ben had threatened anyone. "Oh, my God. That explains it!" I said out loud.

"What does it explain?"

"Well, why did Michelle think that Ben was threatening her? Hani was the only one who asked me if Ben was going to do anything to her in return. He must have told Michelle. And the letter he gave me after he cheated off of me in history? He told me not to talk to anyone about it, that it was personal. He just didn't want people to know how pathetic he is. What a lying bastard!" I was screaming now.

"Natasha, don't give him the satisfaction. Seriously. Don't. Just let it go. You've grown up so much here. Be the bigger person," she begged. She was trying to calm me down, but it was no use. She got me to come inside, and from our room we called Kelsey.

"Natasha, I'm sorry. I warned you he was bad news. I couldn't place why before, but..." Her voice trailed off.

"I know. You can say 'I told you so.' It's all right. I shouldn't have been such an idiot."

"You liked him. That's why it hurts so much. You liked him, he knew it, and he took advantage of you."

"Yeah. He sure did. I wonder if anyone else knows what he's been saying. I'm going to ask around."

"Be careful, Natasha. And Stella's right. Be the bigger person. Don't let him get to you."

"I'll try. I promise." I hung up the phone and looked at Stella.

"Let's get some food," she said. "No one'll be done with work for a few hours. You got out early because of points. I had the second highest number of points, but most everyone else was about even."

We went to Pete's for cheeseburgers, and then we went for a walk. I was amazed how green everything was. It seemed like all of a sudden, Capitol Hill was alive with flowers. Stella and I talked the whole time.

My heart pounded when I thought about how much of a mind fuck Hani had been. I had asked him repeatedly about Michelle, looking for the truth. I would have never snuck down to his room otherwise. I would have never given him my history project. I would have never forgiven him for cheating off of me. From the first day we met, I had thought we shared a connection, one that equaled, if not surpassed, his feelings towards Michelle. I deluded myself time and again. Every time he would smile, my heart would beat a little faster. To find out now that everything I believed about him was a lie, hurt more than anything. I wondered how long he had been lying. I wondered if there was ever any truth to his feelings.

By the time we got back, the others had finished working. I marched into Gretl's room. "Did you guys know he was saying this stuff?"

Cameron shrugged. "I had heard something, but I ignored it. He's so full of shit most of the time I didn't think to pay any attention."

"Same here," Tara agreed. "Besides, you showed us the letter he wrote you when he copied your notebook. It didn't make sense that he would write you all that stuff and then it be you who he said worshiped him or whatever said it was."

"But that's why in the letter he didn't want me talking about it!"

"Yeah, I guess it makes sense now. Man, he's an ass," Tara replied.

"That's what Kelsey said when I told her about it. That he was an ass."

"She's right," Tara nodded. "What do you think, Gretl?"

"If he mentioned your name around me, I just told him to shut up," Gretl said frankly. "So he never got far enough to say that crap. It totally makes sense that he's doing it, though. He's been acting like a jackass for months now. Since the fall pages left."

"I just don't believe him." I shook my head. "But Stella's right. I'm not going to give him the satisfaction. Cameron? Who sits next to you in math class?"

"That girl Mindy. Why, do you want to switch with her? He's always coming over to talk to her before class starts anyway. I'm sure she'd be happy to switch."

For the first time all year, I didn't sit next to Hani in math. He gave me a strange look as Mindy and I switched places. I ignored him. I knew he wouldn't dare challenge it in front of everyone. That would blow his whole image. Later on in the day, he cornered me while I was on a run.

"What happened with math class?" he asked, nudging me with a half smile.

"I wanted a change." I tried to walk away.

"Nat, wait," he started.

I whipped around. "Don't you 'Nat' me. You've been spreading all kinds of rumors behind my back for weeks. Months. Get away from me. I don't want to talk to you." I tried to get away.

"Nat, what are you talking about? Do you have your period or something?"

My eyes blazed. "Oh, you are such a bastard. Leave me alone."

"I never talk about you. Don't you trust me?" Hani tried to take my hand.

I twisted away. "How am I supposed to trust you at all knowing that you've been telling all these lies about me?"

"Nat, you have to understand, I didn't mean anything against you. People are dumb. It's been such a stressful time. I don't know what you are talking about. I need you right now."

"You need me? You need me. What about when I needed you, huh?" My voice was starting to rise.

"I'm there whenever you need me. Don't be so self-centered," he said calmly.

"Me? Self-centered? After all I've done for you, and all you've said about me, how dare you call me self-centered." I felt myself starting to get hysterical. I turned to walk the other direction before I broke down. He came after me.

"This is a really hard time. I told you. Look, can we talk about this? Do I get a chance to defend myself?" Hani stared into my eyes, pleading.

"Well, you can call me later if you want to talk, but I think I'm going to sit next to Cameron in math for a while." I marched off, kicking myself for not being stronger.

Sure enough, he called. He called that night, and every night for two weeks until I finally forgave him.

He never sought me out during the day, and although he was polite enough when other people were around, our conversations were restricted to nighttime after curfew. He kept me on the phone for hours complaining about how everyone was against him and how things with Michelle weren't going so well.

"Then why are you dating her?" I demanded.

"I don't know. I should be dating you, Nat. You are such a great person."

I'm such a chump. I thought, but I said nothing. It was May. We had less than a month left.

Chapter 25: Holes in the Annex

The last few weeks of page life were… tenuous. I went through my daily routine—school, work, home— with a sense of longing. I couldn't wait to leave. Everything in me longed for it. The Clinton Administration was in full swing, and it seemed that everyone was a liberal Democrat. Great for me and my friends, but the rest of my page class seemed to resent it. I wandered through the hallways of health care reform and budget talks, watching the freshman class of congressman fight their way to the forefront of history. Ackerman held a second bagel breakfast, but this time I hurried in, got my food, and moved to the side to sit with my friends. If Brittany thought lox was lobster, I didn't want to know what Stan would say it was.

We got to take a tour of the rotunda. Not a standard tour—we were taken to a corridor that led to a space between the metal shell of the Capitol dome and the old stone façade of the building. They took us up to the statue at the very top, allowing us to stare out at the expanse of city that lay beneath. I held my breath and wished. I wanted to find peace.

Every time I took a run, I concentrated on memorizing every detail around me. I wanted to remember the living history that breathed inside the Capitol. I wanted to remember it independently of my own heartbreak and longing.

Gretl, Cameron, and I decided to spend more time sightseeing around DC. We went to see the AIDS quilt, all the memorials, all the Smithsonians, even the naval academy at Annapolis. We watched *Dances with*

Wolves on the IMAX screen in the Science Museum, and we went paddle-boating to the Jefferson Memorial.

Although I continued to do well in school, I failed my U.S. History Advanced Placement exam. I got a 2. There were loads of questions about wars, none of which I knew anything about.

At the start of the final week, I decided to have some fun with Officer Simpson of the Rayburn subway. Every single time I had delivered flags from Rayburn, he forced me to open every flag box. I went to a toy store and bought a water gun. It was bright green and pink.

I waited around for a flag run. I picked up three flags, and placed the water gun inside one of the boxes.

"Flag boxes, please," he grunted as I edged towards the metal detectors. I handed him my boxes.

He immediately felt that one was heavier than usual. A look of fear crept into his face as he threw open the tampered box. His first instinct was fear, but then he looked closer, picking up the water gun. I looked at him nervously, hoping I hadn't just committed a felony.[**] Silence filled the room.

He started to laugh, for the first time all year. Then everyone—the other officers, other people in line—started laughing.

"Hey, that's a good one!" someone shouted.

Officer Simpson closed the box and shook his head, still laughing. "Serves me right, I guess. Are you one of the pages leaving soon?"

[**] This was a pre-911 world. In this day and age, it probably is a felony to bring a water gun into a house office building.

"This is my last week," I explained.

"Well, young lady, I've been here a long time. Most people are afraid of me. I have to say no one has come up with a prank like this before. Good job. And good luck in the future." He winked at me and patted me on the back.

"Thank you, Officer." I smiled back, took my water gun and flags, and headed back to the House floor.

There was something liberating about his reaction. Somewhere, hidden within the rigid exterior of Capitol Hill, existed a sense of humor.

I told Tara about my prank, and she thought it was hilarious. She had a mischievous twinkle in her eye for the rest of the day.

Tammy and I were in our room packing when Gretl came to tell us about it. "You have to come out and look at the fountain!" she screamed into my room.

"Why? What's happened?" I asked.

"Just come and look!"

Tammy and I raced out with Gretl to the park. The whole fountain was filled with... soapsuds. Hundreds upon hundreds of soapy bubbles. It was getting dark, and the brilliant colors of the sunset twinkled in the bubbles.

"Now who would do a thing like that?" Tara's voice came from behind us. She was standing outside, taking pictures. She winked. Apparently she had decided to play a trick of her own. She had bought several bottles of laundry detergent, and when no one was watching, dumped it in the fountain.

We laughed and sat down on the grass. It had gotten much warmer, but the humidity hadn't hit yet.

Cameron came out a few minutes later with a pizza. We all sat by the soap-sudded fountain, eating and laughing. A few minutes later, some other pages came out to see what was going on.

"That is so wrong. Whoever did that should go to jail." I ignored Michelle's squeaky voice.

"Y'all, this is so disrespectful." Nancy came over to where we were sitting. Michelle was right behind her.

"What is?" I asked innocently. "We're just eating pizza. I've heard that Republicans eat pizza too on occasion."

"Which one of y'all defaced the fountain?" she demanded.

"Defaced it? I don't see any graffiti or anything." Cameron looked at here, wide-eyed.

"Who put the soap in!" She was yelling now.

"I don't know. Why are you asking us? We came out here to have a picnic and it was like that," Tara snapped.

"Y'all are so getting into trouble. Where's Julie?" Michelle retorted. She and Nancy stomped away. Tammy and I exchanged nervous glances.

"I wouldn't worry about it," Tara said, her mouth full of pizza. "If anyone investigates, they'll find a huge empty laundry detergent box in Michelle's closet."

"But we don't know what happened," Cameron reminded her.

"Of course not. I'm just saying that people need to learn to lock their doors." We all laughed. After a few minutes Julie came out. She looked at the fountain and walked over to us.

"What is the meaning of this?"

"Of a picnic?" Tara asked.

"No, of the fountain. In case you girls hadn't noticed, it seems to be a bit soapy."

"Don't look at us, we just came out here to eat. It was like this when we got here." Gretl answered.

"Julie!" Maya had marched out of the building. "I found a large empty box of Tide in Michelle's room. She claims it isn't hers. Would you come inside for a moment?"

Julie raised an eyebrow at us before walking off.

"I guess some people just don't value cleanliness," Gretl sighed. We all laughed again.

"So, the prom is tomorrow night," Cameron said after a few minutes. "Excited?"

"Oh, sure. I love the idea of spending the whole night listening to country music and watching Hani and Michelle make out all night," I responded sarcastically.

"Have you talked to him lately?" Tara asked.

"She talks to him on the phone." Tammy, who had been quietly devouring her pizza, came back to life. I glared at her for revealing my secret. "Then he doesn't talk to her at all during the day."

"Does he call you or do you call him?" Gretl demanded.

"He calls me," I sighed. "He calls and begs me to be his best friend and then gets all stupid when I point out that he's an ass to me in public. He asked me to save him a dance at the prom, but you know that he'll just ignore me."

"Well, we will have a good time. I swear," Gretl stated firmly, "you will ignore him and have fun."

At the dance, I tried to ignore him and have fun. However, when the song, "End of the Road" came on, I decided to try something. I walked over to Hani, who was momentarily not attached to Michelle and tapped him on the shoulder.

"It's our song, remember?"

"What?" he asked.

"From last prom. You said this was our song. Do you want to dance?"

"Oh, yeah. Right. Sure, I'll dance."

We started dancing. It was awkward. He kept making sure that my back was to Michelle. I figured something was going on, and sure enough, before the song ended he excused himself saying that he had to go to the bathroom. I went over to where Stella was standing.

She had her arms folded disapprovingly. "You know he was making faces over your shoulder the whole time," she said frankly.

"Yeah, I figured. But I had to see. He'll call me later, of course, and tell me some bullshit reason why he was doing it. And I'll forgive him because I'm a moron." I sighed.

"If you know what's going on, why do you let him take advantage of you?" Stella demanded angrily.

I looked away, ashamed to say the truth out loud. I looked back into Stella's questioning gaze.

"You're in love with him," she said.

I nodded.

"I'm so sorry, Natasha."

"I know. It's okay." I felt myself on the verge of tears. "I'm going outside for a moment." I spent the rest of the night out on the balcony, staring out into the DC sky. The illuminated silhouette of the Capitol building shone in the evening sky. The twinkling stars took over where the last lit-up window stopped. It was beautiful.

A few days later, we graduated from the page program. I gathered up my belongings, hugged my friends goodbye, and climbed into Chet's van. I had stayed in touch with the Arlington boys even though I didn't see them often. Chet drove me to the airport, where I boarded my plane back to Los Angeles.

By Page

COMMITTEE ON FOREIGN AFFAIRS

RECORD OF RECEIPT

Item(s)
delivered: _____ Meeting notice for Democratic caucus - May 27

Date: May 26, 1993

Delivered by: _____

<table>
<tr><td>OFFICIAL REPORTERS /
<strike>SAMMY DRESSER - 1318</strike></td><td>LONGWORTH</td></tr>
<tr><td>CANTWELL - 1520</td><td>RECEIVED BY: _____</td></tr>
<tr><td>MENENDEZ - 1531</td><td>RECEIVED BY: Mary Edmonds</td></tr>
<tr><td>ENGEL - 1433</td><td>RECEIVED BY: Peter Gutierrez</td></tr>
<tr><td><strike>ROYCE - 1101</strike></td><td>RECEIVED BY: [signature]</td></tr>
<tr><td>BROWN - 1407</td><td>RECEIVED BY: [signature]</td></tr>
<tr><td>_____</td><td>RECEIVED BY: [signature]</td></tr>
<tr><td></td><td>RECEIVED BY: _____</td></tr>
</table>

182

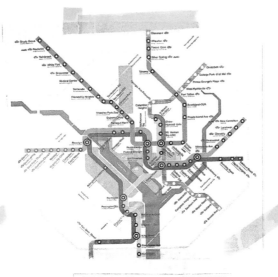

Metro! Goin to Dupont or Pentagon
City.

SEMINARS FOR MEN

Once again the female staff will be offering courses to men of any marital status. Class size will be limited to 18 as course material may prove to be difficult.

101   Combating Stupidity
102   You too can do Housework
103   PMS: Learning to Keep Your Mouth Shut
104   How to Fill an Ice Cube Tray
105   We do Not want sleazy underthings for Christmas (Give Us Money)
106   Understanding the Female Response to You ccoming in drunk at 4:00 AM
107   Wonderful Laundry Techniques (Formerly called "Don't wash my silks")
108   Parenting: No it doesn't end with conception
109   Get a life: Learn how to cook
110   How not to act like an asshole when you're obviously wrong
111   Spelling: Even you can get it right
112   Understanding your financial incompetencies
113   You: The Weaker Sex
114   Reasons to give flowers
115   How to stay awake after sex
116   Why it is unacceptable to relieve yourself anywhere but the bathroom
117   Garbage: Getting it to the curb
118   Sex118A: You can fall asleep without it if you really try
        Sex118B: The morning dilemma: If its "Awake", take a shower
119   The weekend and sports are not synonymous
120   How to put the toilet seat down
121   How to go shopping with your mate and not get lost
122   The remote control: Overcoming your dependency
123   Helpful postural hints for couch potatoes
124   How not to act younger than your children
125   You too can be a designated driver
126   Honest, You don't look like Mel Gibson (especially when naked)
127   Changing your underwear: It really works
128   The attainable goal: Omitting %#@& from your vocabulary
129   Fluffing the blankets after farting is not necessary
130   Real men ask for directions

Please register immediately, as courses are in great demand (as if we had any doubt).

A HEARTBEAT AWAY . . .
. . . QUAYLE OR GORE ?

ELECT CLINTON PRESIDENT

©1992 WILLIAM DAVIS OWEN PUBLISHED BY W. D. OWEN BOX 18767 WASHINGTON D.C. 20036

Clinton for President

Dress Code

for

Pages

OFFICE OF THE DOORKEEPER
U.S. HOUSE OF REPRESENTATIVES
WASHINGTON, D.C.

Best Wishes
Bill and Hillary Clinton

To Naomi Wallace, a great House Page and treasured friend.
Donald K. Anderson
Clerk of the House

Epilogue- Now and Forever

So many people in America never look beyond their front door. They are content to live their lives without recognizing that the country they live in is a collection of differences and similarities. Sometimes those overlap. Mostly, people fail to notice.

At age 16, we all go through tremendous internal change. We begin asking questions and looking outside of ourselves for new answers. Sometimes we find them; sometimes we find new questions.

I keep in touch with many of the pages. Some have started families; others have chosen to go into law or economics. Only a few of us, myself included, rejected politics altogether, choosing instead to live far removed from DC. And even though I've chosen that path, the page program is by far the most life changing, eye opening, and important growing up experience I have ever had. Even though we've all gone in separate directions, the time we spent in Washington is powerful glue that keeps part of each and every one of us bound together. I look at my page friends with love.

I'd like to say that I've forgiven those with whom I was unable to relate. I'd like to say that I've shrugged off their intolerance as teenage ignorance. But I can't. I still remember them with animosity. The power of the page program is as strong as the steel frame that binds the Capitol building. And what we learned—and felt—at 16 stays with us.

The page program is a sampling of America. Blue states, red states. Conservative, liberal, Republican, Democrat. When we exited the microcosm that is the U.S. Congressional Page Program, we took with us our own experiences.

In writing this, I've had to merge some people together for a coherent story, but the experience and events are real, as are the 155 people I met that year. In the years following my tenure, the program changed immensely. Then, in August 2011, the House of Representatives officially abolished the page program. They blamed technology and that the use of emails and smartphones rendered pages redundant. But the fact remains that this 235-year-old tradition was as important to the fabric of congressional tradition as it was to the people who lived it.

2020 Epilogue

Twenty-Eight years ago, I had the unique privilege of spending my junior year of high school in the House of Representatives in Washington DC as a US

House Page. Yesterday, one of the desks we sat behind when on the house floor was used as a barricade.

Although budget cuts and technological advances meant the US House Page Program ended in 2011, there still are Senate Pages and a US Senate Page Program. It's more than likely that those 'Congressional Aids' that saved the Electoral ballots yesterday, included the 16 and 17-year-old Senate Pages who were doing their job and, like me, felt blessed to be part of History.

The year I was a page, Clinton was elected. I remember being on the House floor for his first State of the Union address. I remember going to the Inauguration. I think the fact that one of my favourite parts of that event was being able to attend a special Presidential Gala performance by Fleetwood Mac certainly foreshadowed my later career choices (my year in DC solidified my desire to stay far away from politics.)

That aside, being a Page was a life changing experience which, still to this day, means more to me than I can possibly say. Watching the pictures come out of the Capitol building yesterday, I could only think, If this had happened 28 years ago, I would have been there, locked down in what was meant to be the safest building in the world. Then I thought of those current Senate Pages and wondered how scared their parents must be, wondering if they managed to scurry through the maze of tunnels under the Capitol complex to safety. A maze that is forever imprinted in my memory and my heart.

Pictures below- my page class with Clinton. The riot photo below it in the same place. Then at the overseer desk at our 20-year reunion, below that, the desk used as a barricade yesterday.

About The Author

Originally from Los Angeles, CA, Naomi has been living and working in London since 1999. She has been writing forever and concentrated on theatre in most of her education receiving a BA in Art History and Theatre from Franklin & Marshall in the US, an MFA in Staging Shakespeare from Exeter and a Post Graduate Degree in EU and UK Copyright Law from Kings College in the UK. She is also the author of *Shakespeare's Ripper,* a murder mystery set in London and the play *Madman William* which has received critical acclaim in both the US and UK. She is the co-author of *The Plain and Simple Guide to Music Publishing (UK Edition).*